MW01538424

Inquests and investigations : a practical guide for the use of coroners holding inquests in Ontario : containing all necessary forms : also an Act respecting coroners and coroner's conquests, cap. 23, I Geo. V

Arthur Jukes Johnson

Nabu Public Domain Reprints:

You are holding a reproduction of an original work published before 1923 that is in the public domain in the United States of America, and possibly other countries. You may freely copy and distribute this work as no entity (individual or corporate) has a copyright on the body of the work. This book may contain prior copyright references, and library stamps (as most of these works were scanned from library copies). These have been scanned and retained as part of the historical artifact.

This book may have occasional imperfections such as missing or blurred pages, poor pictures, errant marks, etc. that were either part of the original artifact, or were introduced by the scanning process. We believe this work is culturally important, and despite the imperfections, have elected to bring it back into print as part of our continuing commitment to the preservation of printed works worldwide. We appreciate your understanding of the imperfections in the preservation process, and hope you enjoy this valuable book.

by the Internet Archive in 2008.
From University of Toronto.
be used for non-commercial, personal, research
or educational purposes, or any fair use.
May not be indexed in a commercial service.

INQUESTS AND INVESTIGATIONS

A PRACTICAL GUIDE
FOR THE USE OF CORONERS
HOLDING INQUESTS
IN ONTARIO

Containing all necessary Forms.
Also "An Act Respecting Coroners and
Coroners' Inquests."
Cap. 23, 1 Geo.V.

BY

ARTHUR JUKES JOHNSON
M.B., M.R.C.S. Eng., M.M.C.
Chief Coroner for the
City of Toronto

1911
CANADA LAW BOOK CO., LIMITED
LAW PUBLISHERS
TORONTO

Copyright, Canada, 1911, by
Arthur Jukes Johnson, M.B

INQUESTS AND INVESTIGATIONS

PROCEDURE FOR CORONERS.

When it has been made to appear to a Coroner that an inquiry should be held touching the death of a deceased person, he proceeds as follows:—

1st. He places himself in a position which enables him to control the situation by issuing a warrant (Form No. 1) to take charge of the body, directed to the Chief of Police or Chief Constable of the City, Town, County or District over which his jurisdiction extends, which reads as follows:—

Coroner's Warrant to take Possession of Body.

Province of Ontario of
To wit: } To the Chief Constable of the of in the County (*or* district) of .

By virtue of my office these are in His Majesty's name to charge and command you that on sight hereof you forthwith take in charge the body of , deceased (*or the body of an unknown person*) now lying dead at (*describing as accurately as possible the locality in which body lies*).

1

And thereafter do and execute all such things
as shall be given you in charge on behalf of our
Sovereign Lord the King touching the death of
      , and for so doing this shall be your sufficient
warrant.

Given under my hand and seal this   day
of   , 19   .

Coroner.

In the case of an inquest to be held upon the
body of a person who has died while under
arrest, it will not be necessary to issue Form
No. 1 as the police already have charge of the
body, and as the inquest is compulsory. Form
No. 2 should be issued and the inquiry proceeded with as in all other inquests.

If the body of the deceased has been buried
before the Coroner has issued his warrant to
the police to take possession, it will be necessary to have the body exhumed, and possibly
moved to some convenient place where an
inquest may be held. For this purpose a
"Warrant to take up a body interred" should
be filled out, signed and sealed and given to
the constable to execute. This warrant is as
foll---- -

Warrant to take up a Body Interred.

Province of Canada, | To the Minister and Church-
County of | wardens of (*or* to
To wit: | the proper authorities hav-
| ing charge of the place
| of burial).

Whereas, complaint hath been made unto me, one of His Majesty's Coroners for the said county, on the day of , that the body of one was privately and secretly buried in your township, and that the said died, not of a natural, but violent death; and whereas no notice of the violent death of the said hath been given to any of His Majesty's Coroners for the said county, whereby, on His Majesty's behalf, an inquisition might have been taken on view of the body of the said before his interment, as by law is required. These are, therefore, by virtue of my office, in His Majesty's name, to charge and command you that you forthwith cause the body of the said to be taken up and safely conveyed to , in the said township, that I with my inquest may have a view thereof, and proceed therein according to law. Herein fail not, as you will answer the contrary at your peril.

Given under my hand and seal this day of , one thousand nine hundred and ,

[Seal]

Coroner, County of .

2nd. He proceeds to view the body, and make such further inquiries as he finds necessary to satisfy himself as to whether or not an inquest should be proceeded with.

3rd. If upon this enquiry it is learned that death is purely accidental, or the result of suicide, under circumstances that do not require further investigation, and in which no further facts could be brought to light that would make the cause of death more clear, the Coroner's duty is to collect the evidence connected with the death, enter it in detail on the following form, giving the name and residence of the persons from whom the evidence was obtained, make his affidavit to it, and at once forward it to the Crown Attorney, in the meantime having issued a warrant to bury (Form No. 4). The form to be used is as follows:—

Declaration of Coroner upon Order for Burial.

Dominion of Canada: ⎫ In the matter of ,
Province of Ontario, ⎪ reported by as hav-
County of ⎬ ing been at on
To wit: ⎭ the day of 19 .

I, , Coroner of the in the County of , do solemnly declare that I visited and examined the body of deceased and upon enquiry learned (*here fill in a statement of the facts in detail, and from whom obtained, and state that upon the above facts an order to bury the deceased was gran*

And I make this solemn declaration conscientiously believing it to be true and knowing that it is of the same force and effect as if made under oath and by virtue of the Canada Evidence Act, 1893.

Declared before me at the in the County of , this day of , A.D. 19 .

Coroner, County of

A Commissioner, etc.

Warrant to Bury After a View.

Dominion of Canada: Province of Ontario, County of To wit:

To the Minister and Churchwardens of burying grounds in the of and to all others whom it may concern.

Whereas, an inquisition hath this day been held upon view of the body of who now lies dead in your . These are therefore to certify that you may lawfully permit the body of the said to be buried; and for your so doing this is your warrant.

Given under my hand and seal this day of one thousand nine hundred and

Coroner.

4th. If, however, after having made such enquiry, the Coroner comes to the conclusion that an inquest with a jury is necessary, he proceeds at once to fill out and sign Form No. 2, known as Coroner's Warrant to Hold an Inquest, as follows:—

Coroner's Warrant to Hold Inquest.

Province of Ontario, ⎫ To the Chief Constable of
　County of　　　　 ⎬　the　　 , in the County
　　To wit:　　　　 ⎭　of　　 .

By virtue of my office, these are in His Majesty's name to charge and command you that on sight hereof you summon and warn not less than seven, nor more than twelve able and efficient men of your County personally to be and appear before me, on　　　 , the　　　day of　　　 , at　　　o'clock in the　　　noon of the same day, at the　　　 , called or known by the name or sign of the　　　 , situate in the said County, then and there to do and execute all such things that shall be given them in charge, on behalf of our Sovereign Lord the King, touching the death of　　　 , and for so doing, this shall be your sufficient warrant; and that you also attend at the time and place above mentioned, to make a return of the names of the persons whom you shall have so summoned, and further, to do and execute such other matters as shall be then and there enjoined you, and have you then and there this warrant.

Given under my hand and seal this　　　day of　　　 , 19　.

Coroner.

This warrant must be signed and sealed by the Coroner and given to the police to execute.

5th. At least seven and not more than twelve summonses for the jury should be given to the police with the Coroner's warrant. These are in blank as follows:—

Coroner's Summons to a Juryman.

Province of Ontario, ⎱
    of ⎰
    To wit:

By virtue of a warrant under the hand and seal
of   His Majesty's Coroner for this
you are hereby summoned personally to be and
appear before him as a juryman on the   day
of   , at   o'clock in the
precisely, at the   , known by the name or sign
of   in the   of   then and there
to enquire, on His Majesty's behalf touching the
death of   , and further to do and execute such
other matters and things as shall be then and there
enjoined you, and not depart without leave.

Herein fail not at your peril.

Dated the   day of   , 19 .

To   , of   , in the   .

Constable.

These summonses are filled up by the constable who serves them.

Care should be taken that every juryman
thus served is a ratepayer, and has his name
on the voters' list.

6th. A summons for each witness to be
called must be filled out, signed and sealed
by the Coroner in the following form :—

Summons to a Witness.

Dominion of Canada: ⎫ To   of
    Province of Ontario, ⎪   the   of   ,
        County of   ⎬   in the   of   .
            To wit: ⎭

Whereas I am credibly informed that you can give material evidence on behalf of our Sovereign Lord the King, touching the death of   , now lying dead in the   of   , in the said County of   .

These are, therefore, by virtue of my office, in His Majesty's name, to charge and command you personally to be and appear before me at (*here insert a sufficient description of the place where the inquest is to be held*) in the said   at   of the clock in the   noon, on the   day of   , and then and there to give evidence and be examined, on His Majesty's behalf, before me and my inquest touching the premises.

Given under my hand and seal this   day of   , 19   .

                                        Coroner.

These should be served by the police constable who will later on attend the inquest.

7th. Notify the Crown Attorney as to the time and place at which the inquest has been called and fill up the following statutory d

Declaration of Coroner that Inquest is necessary.

Province of Ontario,
of
To wit:

I, , of the of ,
in the of , a
Coroner in and for said
, do hereby solemnly
declare:

That after viewing the body of (*or* the body of an unknown person) now lying dead at in this , I am of opinion that there is good reason for believing that (*or* an unknown man, woman, or male or female child), now lying dead at did not come to his (*or* her) death from natural causes or from mere accident or mischance; but came to his (*or* her) death from violence or unfair means, or culpable or negligent conduct of others, or under other circumstances requiring investigation by a Coroner's inquest.

And I make this solemn declaration conscientiously believing it to be true and knowing it is of the same force and effect as if made under oath and by virtue of the Canada Evidence Act.

Declared before me at the of
in the of , this
day of , 19 .

Coroner.

A Commissioner, etc.

8th. If a post mortem examination of the body of the deceased is thought necessary, which is generally the case, it should be ordered at the first possible moment. The warrant, Form No. 6, should be filled out, signed and sealed by the Coroner and served

3

by the constable on the legally qualified medical man to whom it is addressed. It is as follows:—

Warrant to Medical Practitioner.

Province of Ontario, ⎫ To   , a legally quali-
          of   ⎬ fied medical practitioner
      To wit: ⎭ of the   of   in
                        the   of   .

By virtue of my office, these are in His Majesty's name to charge and command you that you do (make or assist in making a post mortem examination of the body of   , now lying dead at the   of   in the County of   *without an analysis, and) appear before me and my jury at   in the   of   on the   day of   , 19   , at   o'clock, and give further evidence touching the death of   .

Given under my hand and seal this   day of   , 19   .

Coroner.

The words between the brackets ( ) may be omitted when a post mortem examination is not required.

9th. The report of the post mortem examination must be made out on the form supplied to all Coroners for this purpose, a blank form of which should be attached to

*If an analysis of the contents of the stomach is required

the above warrant (No. 6). This becomes an exhibit to the inquest when presented and reads:—

Exhibit No.
    Referred to by   }
        Dr.

REPORT OF THE POST MORTEM EXAMINATION made upon the body of   , about the age of   , at   , in the County of   , in the Province of Ontario, on the   day of   , 19   , about   hours after death.

Length of body.
Weight.
How nourished.

1. Peculiarities of—
    (*a*) Hair.
    (*b*) Teeth.
    (*c*) Eyes.
    (*d*) Scars, etc.
2. Rigor Mortis.
3. Post mortem staining.
4. Decomposition.
5. Marks of external violence.

INTERNAL EXAMINATION.

6. *Chest*—
    (*a*) Height of Diaphragm in Infants.
    (*b*) Pericardium.

7. *Heart*—Size and weight.
    (*a*) Right Auricle—contents.
    (*b*) Tricuspid Valve and Orifice.
    (*c*) Right Ventricle—contents.
    (*d*) Pulmonary Orifice and Valve.
    (*e*) Left Auricle—contents.
    (*f*) Mitral Orifice and Valve.
    (*g*) Left Ventricle—contents.
    (*h*) Aortic Orifice and Valve.

8. Aorta and Large Vessels.

9. Coronary Arteries.

10. Condition of Heart Muscle.

11. Mouth.

12. Tongue.

13. Aesophagus.

14. Larynx.

15. Trachea.

16. Bronchi.

17. Thyroid.

18. Thymus.

19. Pleurae—
    (*a*) Right.
    (*b*) Left.

20. Lungs—
    (*a*) Right.
    (*b*) Left.

21. *Abdomen*—Peritoneum, etc.

22. Stomach and contents.

23. Intestines and Mesenteric Glands.

24. Liver—
    (*a*) Surface.
    (*b*) Section.
    (*c*) Weight.

2

26. Spleen.
27. Pancreas.
28. Kidneys and Ureters—
    (*a*) Right.
    (*b*) Left.
    (*c*) Suprarenal Bodies.
29. Bladder and contents.
30. Generative Organs—in the female—
    (*a*) Uterus.
    (*b*) Ovaries and Tubes.
31. *Head*—
    (*a*) Scalp.
    (*b*) Meninges and Blood Vessels.
32. Brain—
    (*a*) Hemisphere.
    (*b*) Ventricles.
    (*c*) Cornua.
    (*d*) Pons.
    (*e*) Cerebellum.
    (*f*) Medulla.
33. Spinal Cord.

Blank forms of the above may be obtained from the Deputy Attorney-General's Department, Parliament Buildings, Toronto.

10th. If, from the circumstances of the case, it is deemed advisable that the evidence or any part of it should be taken in shorthand, the Coroner must obtain the sanction of the Crown Attorney first and then notify a stenographer that he will be required at

the time and place where the inquest is to
be held for this purpose.

Before the opening of the inquest, if the
Coroner learns that an arrest has been made
in the matter of the inquest about to be held,
it is advisable that the prisoner should be
present at the inquest. The Coroner should,
therefore, issue his warrant to have the prisoner brought up from the gaol that he may
be present at the inquest, this should read
as follows:—

Warrant to Bring Prisoner from Gaol.

To the keeper of His Majesty's gaol at
in the County of   .

Whereas you have in your custody the body of
      charged with the murder of   .

These are by virtue of my office to command
you forthwith to deliver the said   into the
hands of the police officer,   , that the said
      may be present at my inquest now being
held upon the body of   .

Herein fail not at your peril.

Given under my hand and seal this   day
of   , 19   .

                              Coroner.

Before going to an inquest the Coroner
should see that he has with him convenient
wr   a box

of small adhesive seals, some double sheets of foolscap, together with certain forms.

These forms are:—

First. *A binder-sheet.*—This should consist of a double sheet of good, strong foolscap, upon which the inquest should be written.

On the front of the first page of this write "The Caption" or "Incipitur"; the names of the jurymen; the verdict, followed by the attestation and the signatures of the Coroner and jurors:—

Dominion of Canada: ⎫
  Province of Ontario, ⎪
    County of ⎬
      To wit: ⎭

An inquisition indented taken for our Sovereign Lord the King, at the house of   , known by the sign of   , situate in the   of   , in the County of   , on the   day of   , in the *   year of the reign of our Sovereign Lord King George V., before   , Esquire, one of the said Coroners of our said Lord the King, for the said county, on view of the body of   , then and there lying dead, upon the oath of (*insert names of jurymen one below the other*) good and lawful men of the said county, duly chosen, and who being then and there duly sworn and charged to enquire for our Lord the King, when, where,

*King George V ascended the Throne, May 6th, 1910.

how, and by what means the said   came to
death, do upon their oath say : That

.

(here insert verdict)

In witness whereof, as well the said Coroner as
the said jurors aforesaid have hereunto set and subscribed their hands and seals the day and year first
above written. (*Coroner signs first, then the Foreman, then all the jury, one below the other.*)

It may not be possible to get all this on
the front of the first page, if not, it should be
continued on the reverse of this page and so,
if necessary, on to the third page.

The advantage of this double sheet is, that
as all the evidence is written on one side only
of sheets of foolscap, these may all be enclosed
in this double sheet when the papers are sent
to the County Crown Attorney or clerk of the
peace. Sheets of this kind already printed
may now be obtained, and are a great con-
venience. (See Form No. 15.)

Second. *Information of Witnesses.*—This
should constitute the first of the single sheets
on which the evidence is to be taken, and is
partly printed as follows :—

Information of Witnesses.

Dominion of Canada:
  Province of Ontario,
    County of
      To wit:

Information of witnesses severally taken and acknowledged on behalf of our Sovereign Lord the King touching the death of   at the known by the name or sign of   , in the of   , in the County of   , on the day of   , in the year of our Lord one thousand nine hundred and   , before me,   , one of His Majesty's Coroners for the said   , on an inquisition then and there taken, on view of the body of the said   , then and there lying dead, as follows, to wit: I   , of the   of   , in the said County of   , being sworn, saith:

Third.

Warrant to Bury After a View.

Province of Ontario,
  of
    To wit:

To the person in charge or control of the burying grounds in the and to all others whom it may concern.

Whereas, an inquisition hath this day been held upon view of the body of   , who now lies dead in your (township *or* city *or as the case may be*). These are therefore to certify that you may lawfully permit the body of the said   to be buried; and for your so doing this is your warrant.

Given under my hand and seal this   day of   , 19   .

Coroner.

Fourth. Warrant to apprehend the accused as follows:—

Warrant to Apprehend the Accused.

Canada:
Province of Ontario,
County of
To wit:

To the Constables of the Township of   , in the County of   , and all other His Majesty's peace officers in the said County.

Whereas, by an inquisition taken before me,   , one of His Majesty's Coroners for the said County, this   day of   , at   , in the said County, on view of the body of   , then and there lying dead, one (*insert name of person to be arrested*), late of (*insert address of same*), in the said county (*insert occupation*), stands charged with the wilful murder of the said (*insert name of deceased—or if the offence is contempt of Court, then state this*).

These are therefore, by virtue of my office, in His Majesty's name, to charge and command you and every of you, that you or some or one of you, without delay, do apprehend and bring before me,   , the said Coroner, or one of His Majesty's justices of the peace of the said County, the body of the said (*insert name of person to be apprehended*), of whom you shall have notice, that he may be dealt with according to law; and for your so doing this is your warrant.

Given under my hand and seal this   day of   , one thousand nine hundred and   .

The accused here referred to may not always be the person who is found guilty by the jury of a murder or manslaughter.

This form may be used to arrest anyone who behaves in such a way as to interrupt the holding of the Coroner's court, or who commits any wrongful act with the object of casting contempt upon the judicial proceedings of the inquest.   It may be used also to arrest any witness upon whom a subpœna has been served, and who without justification refuses to attend the inquest, or to reply to the Coroner's questions.

Fifth. A few of Form No. 8, "Summons to a witness," in case he has to call a witness not already served:—

Summons to a Witness.

Province of Ontario, ⎫ To   , of the
        of   ⎬ of   , in the
    To wit: ⎭ of   .

Whereas I am credibly informed that you can give material evidence on behalf of our Sovereign Lord the King, touching the death of   , now lying dead in the   of   , in the said County of   .   These are, therefore, by virtue of my office, in His Majesty's name, to charge and command you personally to be and appear before me at (*here insert a sufficient description of the*

place where the inquest is to be held) in the said
            at   of the clock in the   noon,
on the   day of   , and then and there to
give evidence and be examined, on His Majesty's
behalf, before me and my inquest touching the
premises.

Given under my hand and seal this   day
of   , 19   .

Coroner.

Sixth. A form of recognizance to be used in
case an adjournment becomes necessary, as
follows:—

Recognizance before Coroner.

Province of Ontario,

Be it remembered, that
and
of the same place,
do severally
acknowledge to owe to our Sovereign Lord the
King the sum of   Dollars each of lawful
money of Canada, to be levied on their several
goods and chattels, lands and tenements, by way of
recognizance, to His Majesty's use, in case default
shall happen to be made in the condition hereunder
written.

The condition of this recognizance is such, that
if the above bounden   and
do severally personally appear at the next general
gaol delivery to be holden in and for the county of
            , and the said   shall then and
there prefer, or cause to be preferred to the grand
jury, a bill of indictment against   late
of   and now in custody for the
of

and   do then and there severally
personally appear to give evidence upon such bill
of indictment to the said grand jury; and in case
the said bill of indictment be found by the grand
jury a true bill, that then the said   and
        do severally personally appear at the said
general gaol delivery, and the said   shall
then and there prosecute the said   on such
indictment, and the said   and   do
then and there severally give evidence to the jury
that shall pass on the trial of the said
touching the premises, and in case the said bill of
indictment shall be returned not found, that they
do severally personally appear at the said general
gaol delivery, and then and there prosecute and
give evidence to the jury that shall pass on the trial
of the said   upon an inquisition taken
before me, one of His Majesty's Coroners for the
said   on view of the body of the said   ,
and not depart the Court without leave, then this
recognizance to be void, otherwise to remain in full
force.

Taken and acknowledge this   day of   ,
before me,

Coroner.

Seventh. Pay list for jurors. The following
is the form generally used :—

Order for Payment of Jurors.

In the matter of the inquest upon
        I,   , an associate Coroner in and for the
        of   , do hereby certify that the persons
whose names appear in the first column of the
following schedule, who reside at the respective
places named in the second column thereof, actually sat as jurors upon the inquest held by me as

Coroner upon the body of   , deceased, on the
                              day of   ,
A.D. 19   , and that the time occupied by such inquest was as follows:

and that the said jurors are entitled to mileage in
the number of miles set opposite their names in the
third column of the said schedule, and are respectively entitled to the sums set opposite their names
in the fourth column of the said schedule, to compensate them for their fees and mileage pursuant
to the Act fifty-ninth, Victoria, chapter 25, entitled
"An Act respecting the Fees of Jurors at Coroner's Inquests."

To the treasurer of the

                                        Coroner.

SCHEDULE ABOVE REFERRED TO.

1	2	3	4	We, the undersigned, acknowledge receipt of the amounts payable to us at the date set opposite to our respective signatures.	Date of Payment.
NAMES OF JURORS.	ADDRESS.	Mileage.	Amount Payable.		
1.					
2.					
3.					
4.					
5.					
6.					
7.					
8.					
9.					
10.					
11.					
12.					

THE INQUEST.

THE OPENING OF THE INQUEST.

At the hour specified on the Coroner's warrant at which the inquest is to open the Coroner should be in his place, ready to proceed.

The constable who has summoned the jury should be present and have with him the names and addresses of the jurymen whom he has served together with the Coroner's warrant on the authority of which he has collected them.

The warrant is returned to the Coroner, who then proceeds to open his Court by saying:

"You good men of this county (or city, as the case may be) summoned to appear here this day, to inquire for our Sovereign Lord the King when, where, how, and by what means (*name of deceased, or unknown man, woman or child*) came to his (*or her*) death, answer to your names as you shall be called, every man at the first call, upon the pain and peril that shall fall thereon."

The name of each member of the jury is now called and if seven or more answer they will constitute the jury. Care should be taken that the jury is composed of ratepayers in the municipality (R.S.O. 1897, c. 97, s. 8), and that no member is an interested party in the proceedings.

The Coroner now asks the jury to select their foreman, which if they hesitate to do the Coroner should request the man he thinks most fitted to perform the duties to act.

This juror is asked to stand up and take the Bible in his right hand and listen to his oath, and the jury at the same time are bidden to harken to their foreman's oath. The oath is then delivered to the foreman as follows:—

"You shall diligently inquire and true presentment make of all such matters and things as shall here be given you in charge on behalf of our Sovereign Lord the King, touching the death of ———, now lying dead, of whose body you shall have the view; you shall present no man for hatred, malice or illwill; nor spare any through fear, favour or affection; but a true verdict give according to the evidence and the best of your skill and knowledge. So help you God."

After the foreman has kissed the Bible it is handed to the constable in charge of the jury who gives it thereafter to the jurors as they come to be sworn.

It is not necessary to swear each of the jury-men separately. After the foreman is sworn he should take his seat at the end of the first row of the jury benches and the Coroner calls the names of three jurors. Standing up they take the Bible in their right hands and the Coroner says:—

"The oath which your foreman upon this inquest hath now taken before you on his part, you, and each of you, are severally well and truly to observe and keep on your parts. So help you God."

Each juror kisses the Bible and then takes his seat. The same oath is administered to the balance of the jury, three at a time, until they are all sworn.

The Coroner, to be certain that his jury is all properly sworn, proceeds to call over the names of the jury as follows:—

"Gentlemen of the jury, answer to your names as they shall be called, and if you are sworn say 'sworn.'"

The oath to the foreman and jury may be administered *super visum corporis,* but where this has not been done as soon as the jury is sworn the Coroner should tell them that their first duty is to view the body, and the Coroner

3

must be present and view the body with the
jury.   Care should be taken that the view is
made **after** the jury is sworn and not *before.*

If there are wounds on the body the Coroner may call the attention of the jury to them,
as well as explain, where a post mortem has
been made, what marks have been made on the
body in the course of such an examination.

After the body has been viewed the Coroner
and jury proceed to the room in which the evidence is to be heard.   As soon as the jury is
seated the Coroner calls the name of each juror,
beginning with the foreman, and if they are all
present he may now proceed to examine the
witnesses.

If he has not already done so the Coroner
should now arrange the papers which he will
require in the taking of evidence.   The form
headed, "Information of Witnesses," will be
the first used.   This may be filled in down to
the space for the name of the first witness.
Other sheets of foolscap should be arranged on
which the evidence which has been begun on
the form may be continued.   Evidence should
be written on one side of a sheet of foolscap
only, and a margin an inch and a half or two

inches wide should be left on the left-hand side of the page.

If the foolscap is not marked with a line dividing this margin from the ruled part of the paper, an easy method of running a line as required is to double the left-hand margin of the sheet over onto the sheet and run the finger nail down it; in this way when the sheet is smoothed out a crease is left which is a very good guide in beginning each line.

Where the Coroner, with the sanction of the Crown Attorney, has arranged that all or any part of the evidence be taken in shorthand, the stenographer appointed by the Coroner for this purpose, shall now, before any evidence is taken, be sworn as follows:—

"You swear that you will to the best of your skill and ability, well and faithfully, take down the evidence in this case and truly transcribe the same without favour or affection, prejudice or partiality, to any of the parties. So help you God."

Where the evidence is taken in shorthand, the procedure will be changed in so far as refers to the recording of the evidence only. Evidence taken in this way need not be read over to the witness, nor will it be necessary for

the witness to sign anything. It will be sufficient if the transcript of the evidence, when
typewritten by the stenographer, is signed by
the Coroner and is accompanied by an affidavit
of the stenographer that it is a true report of
the evidence.

Each witness is sworn, examined and cross-
examined in precisely the same manner as
occurs when the evidence is taken down by
the Coroner (see page 30).

The typewritten transcript of the evidence
should be enclosed in the inquest proper
(which has been written on the binder-sheet),
and with the exhibits sent to the Crown Attorney or clerk of the peace as described at
page 41.

Except when a stenographer is employed,
all depositions should be taken in the Coroner's
own handwriting, and written in ink.

Abbreviations and figures should not be
used.

It is advisable to take down the evidence of
each witness in the first person and to use, if
possible, the exact "words used by the witness."

In case a witness does not speak the Eng-
lish language, the Coroner may, if he thinks
nec   Crown

Attorney, employ an interpreter, to whom the following oath shall be administered : —

"You shall well and truly interpret unto the several witnesses here produced on behalf of our Sovereign Lord the King touching the death of   , the oath that shall be administered unto them, and also the questions and demands which shall be made to the witnesses by the Court or the jury concerning the matter of this inquiry, and you shall well and truly interpret the answers which the witnesses shall hereunto give, according to the best of your skill and ability. So help you God."

All letters, documents, bottles, instruments, etc., referred to by a witness, if forming a part of an inquest, are kept as exhibits and should be referred to by number. They should be marked "Exhibit No.   ," referred to by in his (*or* her) evidence and initialled by the Coroner.

It is advisable to make the *report* of the post mortem an exhibit of the inquest.

The first witness should be the constable who summoned the jury; enter his name on the sheet already partly filled up and headed "Information of Witnesses," in the space begin-

ning, "I   ," and fill in the city, town or
village and the county.   He should then be
sworn as follows:—

"The evidence that you shall give to this
inquest on behalf of our Sovereign Lord the
King touching the death of   shall be
the truth, the whole truth and nothing but
the truth. So help you God."

This witness should be asked as to the summoning of the jury, on whose order? if they are
all qualified to act as jurors, etc? He should
also put on record the fact that the body of
deceased was viewed by the jury and the Coroner. If he knows anything about the circumstances connected with the death of the deceased he can give this now or be recalled by
the Coroner at a more convenient time. When
witness has told his story the foreman and the
jury should be asked if they have any questions
to ask the witness; if so the questions should be
given to the Coroner and the Coroner should
ask the witness.

If the County Crown Attorney is present,
he should now have the privilege of examining
or cross-examining the witness. But if the
Attorney-General is represented by special
coun̄sel at the inquest this gentleman takes the

place of the Crown Attorney and should have
every facility given to him to enable him to
examine or cross-examine the several witnesses.
It must be remembered that, under these circumstances, although the special counsel and
the Crown Attorney may both be present at an
inquest, it is not contemplated that they should
both examine or cross-examine any witness.
The examination by one is all that is expected.

When the counsel for the Crown has
finished with a witness, the counsel appearing
for anyone interested in the proceedings has,
with the consent of the Coroner, the same
privileges which were accorded to the Crown.
If the County Crown Attorney or his represen-
tative is not present, no counsel should be allowed to examine or cross-examine a witness,
the Coroner doing all this himself, although
a counsel may, from time to time, suggest
to the Coroner any question he wishes to have
asked.

A prisoner, who is present at an inquest,
has the right to give evidence in his own behalf
if he *so desires*. He should be warned (see
Form No. 67). If he does give his evidence
he can be subjected to cross-examination and
cannot refuse to answer any question put to

him relevant to the case. If the question tends to incriminate him, he has the right to object to answer on that ground. If he takes the objection he is protected, and the evidence cannot be used against him in a future trial.

The evidence, when taken down by the Coroner, is read over to the witness, and after correcting any inaccuracies, if such exist, the witness signs it. The Coroner adds the attestation, which should be written partly on the left-hand margin and partly on the body of the sheet of fooscap as follows:—

Taken upon oath and acknowledged
 this day of in the year   *(Signature*
of our Lord one thousand nine   *of witness.*
hundred and , before me.

   Coroner for the County of   .

In this way the end of the evidence of one witness and the beginning of that of the next is so definitely marked that it can be found very easily.

Every witness is called and examined in the same manner, and it is to be remembered that all evidence that is relevant both for the Crown and for the defence should be taken.

When it is impossible to finish all the evidence at one sitting, or if "in the sound discretion and judgment of the Coroner" for any other cause an adjournment becomes necessary, the Coroner may order an adjournment to a future day, at the same or some other place if more convenient.

Under these circumstances the Coroner should tell the jury that it will be impossible to close the inquest at that sitting, and explain why. They should be then asked to say when they will be prepared to meet again to hear further evidence. The Coroner may suggest a date when the balance of the evidence will be available, and a date may in this way be arrived at which will be convenient to all parties concerned. As soon as the date and place at which the adjourned inquest is to meet is decided on, the Coroner should take the recognizance of the jurors to attend at the time and place so appointed. This is done by the Coroner addressing the jury as follows:—

"Gentlemen: You acknowledge yourselves severally to owe to our Sovereign Lord the King the sum of one hundred dollars to be levied on your goods and chattels, lands and tenements for His Majesty's use

upon condition that if you and each of you
personally appear here again (*or* at an adjourned place) on   next, being the
          day of   instant, at   of
the clock in the   precisely, then and
there to make further inquiry on behalf of
our said Sovereign Lord the King, touching
the death of the said   , of whose body
you have had the view; then this recognizance to be void, or else to be in full force.
Are you content?"

The witnesses should be notified at the same
time as to when and where the adjourned inquest will be proceeded with and instructed
to attend. The jury is then dismissed by the
Coroner saying :—

"Gentlemen : The Court doth dismiss you
for this time, but requires you severally to
appear here again (*or* at the adjourned
place) on   . the   day of   ,
instant, at   of the clock, in the
precisely, upon pain of one hundred dollars
a man, on the condition in your recognizance
entered into."

In case a prisoner who has been present at
an inquest has to be held pending a further
sess.... of .... .ck to

gaol the officer in charge of him should be with him and give to the keeper of the gaol a warrant of detainer as follows:—

Warrant of Detainer.

Province of Canada: To the keeper of His Ma-
   County of   jesty's gaol at   ,
     To wit: of the County of   .

Whereas you have in your custody the body of (*here insert name of prisoner*), and whereas by an inquisition taken before me, one of His Majesty's Coroners for the said County of   , the day and year hereunder written, at the   of in the said county, on view of the body of (*here insert name of deceased*) then and there lying dead, he, the said (*here insert name of prisoner*) stands charged with (*here insert the crime charged*).

These are, therefore, in His Majesty's name, by virtue of my office, to charge and command you to detain and keep in your custody the body of the said (*here insert name of prisoner*) until he shall thence be discharged by due course of law; and for your so doing this is your warrant.

Given under my hand and seal this   day of   , one thousand nine hundred and   ,
                      Coroner, County of   .

THE INQUEST REASSEMBLES AFTER ADJOURNMENT.

At the hour appointed for the jury to reassemble after adjournment the Coroner should open his Court by making the following pro-clamation :—

"Oyez, Oyez, Oyez. All manner of persons who have anything more to do at this Court before the King's Coroner for this county, on this inquest now to be taken and adjourned over to this time and place, draw near and give your attendance; and you, gentlemen of the jury, who have been empanelled and sworn upon this inquest to inquire into the death of   , severally answer to your names and save your recognizances."

Call the name of each juryman, beginning with the foreman, and if the foreman and six men answer proceed to take the next witness. Any juryman who comes in late or who absents himself should have his name and address sent to the County Crown Attorney, that his fine may be estreated at the next Court of competent jurisdiction.

If the foreman and six men do not answer when called the inquest must be adjourned until they are present.

When all the witnesses have been examined an' before closing the Coroner should make a proclamation for the attendance of witnesses as follows :—

"If there is any other person who can give further evidence on behalf of our Sovereign Lord the King as to when, where, how and by what means,   came to his death, let him come forward and he shall be heard."

If there is no further evidence the Coroner proceeds to address the jury.

In doing this he should endeavour to give a resumé of all the evidence.

The law applicable to the case under consideration should be explained; quotations from the Criminal Code being read if necessary.

Remind the jury of their oath; that they are sworn to enquire when, where, how and by what means the deceased came to his or her death, and that their verdict must be given "upon the evidence" and see that the verdict is definite on these points as far as possible. The jury should be told that the evidence as taken down will be left in the room with them in case they should wish to refer to it, and that the Coroner may be summoned by them to explain any point that they do not understand.

If the jury is to remain in the room in which the evidence has been taken the constable should be instructed to clear the room, every one being put out except the jury.

The constable who has charge of the jury should then be sworn as follows:—

"You shall well and truly keep the jury upon this inquiry without meat, drink or fire; you shall not suffer any person to speak to them, nor shall you speak to them yourself, unless it be to ask them if they have agreed on their verdict, until they shall be agreed. So help you God."

After the constable has cleared the room he should remain outside, but near the door, that he may be easily summoned by the foreman when required.

When the jury have agreed on their verdict, word is taken to the Coroner by the constable in charge; upon this the Coroner returns to the jury-room and having resumed his seat asks: "Gentlemen of the jury, have you decided upon your verdict?" The foreman thereupon hands him the written verdict which he reads aloud, and after asking any questions that he may think necessary to enable him to thoroughly un........................ds to enter it in proper legal form in the part reserved for this purpose at the foot of the first page, and the top of the second of the binder-sheet referred to at page 61 (see forms of verdict, pages 73 to 107). This being finished he addresses the jury as follows:—

"Gentlemen of the jury: Harken to your verdict as delivered by you and as I have recorded it. You find that (here repeat the wording of the verdict) and add, 'so say you all.'"

The verdict when entered is followed by the attestation, "In witness whereof as well the Coroner as the jury aforesaid have hereunto set and subscribed their hands and seals the day and date last above written." The Coroner signs his name first, adding "Coroner," and is followed by the foreman and then all the jurors. A seal should be affixed after the Coroner's name, and after the name of each juryman. When all have signed the Coroner addresses the jury as follows:—

"Oyez, Oyez, Oyez. All you good men of this County summoned to appear here this day to enquire for our Sovereign Lord the King as to when, where, how and by what means   came to his (or her) death

depart now and take your ease. God save
the King."

Before the jury leaves the room it is well
for the Coroner to tell them when and where
they are to apply for their fees and warn them
that in making application to the treasurer
each one is expected to shew his summons for
the purpose of identification.

The "Order for Payment of Jurors" (see
Form No. 17, page 21) should be filled out on
one of the forms obtainable for this purpose,
as soon as possible after the close of the inquest and given to the county or city treasurer, as the case may be. On it is entered
the name and address of each juror with the
amount payable to each. This amount is made
up of mileage at the rate of ten cents a mile
one way for every mile necessarily travelled;
together with the sum of one dollar for every
sitting of the inquest of four hours or less.
If any one sitting of the inquest extends over
this time, it must be divided into one sitting of
four hours, and one for the balance, constitut-
ing in reality two sittings.

A "Warrant to bury the body after a view"
(No. 4) should be signed at the close of the
i   s been

viewed by the jury as the Coroner may think advisable, and given to the friends of the deceased or to the police.

In the case of an unclaimed body notice must be sent to the Inspector of Anatomy within twenty-four hours. He is supplied with forms, one of which should be signed by the Coroner; this liberates the body from the control of the Coroner. It is usual also for the Coroner to sign the death certificate required by the Medical Health Department which should be given to the friends of the deceased.

At the **close of the inquest** the Coroner may certify to the account of the medical man who made the post mortem (Form No. 24).

As soon after the inquest is completed as possible all the depositions together with the finding of the jury, etc., and all exhibits and any other matters pertaining to the inquest must be sent to the County Crown Attorney for the county in which the inquest was held. On the filing of the inquest papers the Crown Attorney issues to the Coroner a certificate of acceptance. This certificate, which is in duplicate, the Coroner attaches to his account (which is always to be made in duplicate) for the holding of the inquest and forwards it to

4

The coroner sends his office in duplicate at the close of the inquest to

the clerk of the peace for the city or county in which the inquest was held, before the first day of the next quarter.

If the verdict, when returned, implicates anyone as causing the death of the deceased, the Coroner should at once make out his warrant for the arrest of such person and give it to the constable to execute. This can conveniently be done while the jury are signing their verdict.

The form for this will be found on page 18.

The constable on duty at the inquest takes this warrant, and a certificate of the finding of the jury, to his station, or chief, as the case may be.

The form of the certificate in general use is:—

Inquest on the body of   held at   , in the County of   , on the   day of   , 19   .

Verdict: Murder against   ,

M.D.,
Coroner, County of   .

OF THE INQUEST ON EXECUTED CRIMINALS.

Where the execution of a criminal has taken place at any gaol or prison, an inquest is compulsory

As soon as the Coroner is notified that the execution has taken place and that there is a body upon which an inquest is to be held, he at once issues his warrant (Form No. 2), together with the other necessary papers for the inquest. This should be done as soon after the execution has taken place as it reasonably can.

It will be remembered that it is now necessary to have the jury composed altogether of ratepayers and not, as was formerly the custom, half the jury only being taken from the voters' list and the other half being composed of prisoners. No officer or employee or inmate of the institution, in which the deceased died, can be on the jury.

The finding of the jury in these cases is made out in duplicate. Make out two complete sheets, Form No. 15, and have them both signed. One copy of this is given to the keeper of the gaol that it may be exposed for twenty-four hours on the door of the gaol in which the execution took place.

The inquest in these cases should read as follows:—

Canada:
Province of Ontario,
County of
        To wit:

King George came to the Throne May 6. 1910

An inquisition taken for our Sovereign Lord
the King, at the gaol or prison known by the
name of   , situate in the   of   ,
in the County of   on the   day of
       , 19   , in the   year of the reign
of our Sovereign Lord George V., before   ,
Esquire, one of the Coroners of our said Lord
the King, for the said county, on view of the
body of   , then and there lying dead, upon
the oath (*or* oath and affirmation) of
(*naming all the jurors sworn*) good and lawful men
of the said county, duly chosen, and who being then
and there duly sworn, and charged to inquire for
our said Lord the King, when, where, how and by
what means the said   came to his death, do
upon their oath say: That the said   , being a
prisoner confined in the common gaol for the
County of   , under legal sentence that he be
hanged by the neck until he be dead, was, on
       day, the   day of   , A.D. 19   ,
within the walls of the said gaol, legally hanged
by the neck until he was dead, in pursuance and
in accordance with such sentence; and the jury
aforesaid, upon their oath aforesaid, do say, that
having enquired into the identity of the body, of
which they have had a view, and upon which this
inquest has been held, with that of the said prisoner
       , so under sentence of death as aforesaid,
they have ascertained the identity of the same, and
that judgment of death was duly executed upon the
said offender. And the jurors aforesaid, upon their
oath aforesaid, do further say, that the said   ,
in   and by the means aforesaid, came to his
de

In witness whereof, as well the said Coroner as the jurors aforesaid, have hereunto set and subscribed their hands and seals the day and year first above written.

Investigation of Fires.

Where a Coroner is asked to investigate the cause or origin of a fire that has occurred within his jurisdiction, he can only do so in one of two ways. *First,* by his receiving a requisition in writing, signed by the authorized agent of an insurance company, in which he sets forth the facts of the case as far as known, together with the statutory declaration that the statements are true; or *secondly,* by a resolution passed by the council for the city, town, village, or township, in which the fire took place, that there are proper reasons for such an investigation, and stating such reasons.

In either case he must also have an undertaking on the part of the insurance company or council to pay the expenses of the enquiry.

These preliminaries having been arranged, it should be determined by mutual agreement between the parties requiring the inquest, and the Coroner, whether the inquiry should be held with or without a jury. If it is decided to

hold the inquiry with a jury, then Form No.
2 should be issued, changing the wording in a
way to suit the circumstances. Not less than
seven nor more than twelve jurors should be
sworn to inquire when, how, where, and by
what means this fire occurred. The rest of the
procedure is practically the same as that which
takes place where an inquest is held upon a
dead body. The witnesses are all sworn and
examined in the same way.

As the examination is generally rather tech-
nical in these cases, it is advisable that who-
ever asks for the investigation should under-
take to provide a stenographer.

If an inquiry is held without a jury, the
evidence is taken in the same way as if a jury
were present. The Coroner's verdict on the
evidence will be signed by himself only.

Fees allowed in a fire inquest are ten dollars, and if the inquiry extends beyond one
day, then ten dollars a day for each of two days
thereafter, and no more, but no adjournment
can be charged for unless the Coroner has certified, under his hand, why and for what purpose, in his opinion, an adjournment took place
or became necessary. (R.S.O. 1897, c. 275, s.
10.)

Form for the caption to be used in a fire inquest is as follows:—

                Canada:
          Province of Ontario,
           County of
              To wit:

The inquisition taken for our Sovereign Lord the King, at the house of   known by the sign of   situate in the   of   in the County of   on the   day of   in the   year of the reign of our Sovereign Lord George the Fifth, before   , Esquire, one of the Coroners of our Lord the King for the said county, to inquire into the cause or origin of a certain fire which occurred in the said   of   on the   day of   , A.D. 19   , in the said   year of the reign of our Sovereign Lord George V., at or about the hour of   o'clock in the   noon, whereby the   of   situate upon lot No.   on the   side of   street in the said   of   in the said county of   was   consumed or damaged, upon the oath (or affirmation) of (*insert names of jurors*) good and lawful men of the said   duly chosen from among the householders resident in the vicinity of the said fire; and who, being then and there duly sworn and charged to inquire, for our said Lord the King, into the cause or origin of said fire, and whether it was kindled by design or was the result of negligence or accident, do upon their oaths say that,

(*here insert verdict and close with the attestation used in the case of an inquest held on a dead body*)

—like the binder-sheet spoken of at page— the above should be written on the outside of a double sheet of foolscap paper, which will act as a cover for the sheets of paper on which the evidence has been taken.

See 1 George V. ch. 23, secs. 26 to 31 inclusive, Part III. re Investigation of Fires to be found at page 120.

FORMS

FOR

WARRANTS, ORDERS, SCHEDULE OF FEES, ETC.

FORM No. 1.

Coroner's Warrant to Take Possession of Body.

Province of Ontario, ⎧ To the Chief Constable of
of ⎨ the   of   in the
To wit: ⎩ County (*or* district) of .

By virtue of my office these are in His Majesty's name to charge and command you that on sight hereof you forthwith take in charge the body of , deceased (*or* the body of an unknown person) now lying dead at (*describing as accurately as possible the locality in which body lies*).

And thereafter do and execute all such things as shall be given you in charge on behalf of our Sovereign Lord the King touching the death of , and for so doing this shall be your sufficient warrant.

Given under my hand and seal this day of , 19 .

Coroner.

FORM No. 2.

Warrant to Hold Inquest on Death.

Province of Ontario, ⎧ To the Chief Constable of
of ⎨ the   of   in the
To wit: ⎩ County (*or* district) of .

By virtue of my office these are in His Majesty's name to charge and command you that on sight hereof you summon and warn   (*not less than* seven *nor more than* twelve) able and efficient men of your county (*or* city) personally to be and appear before me on   day the   day of   at   o'clock in the   noon of the same day at   , called or known by the name or sign of   , situate in the said   then and there to do and execute all such things that shall be given them in charge on behalf of our Sovereign Lord the King touching the death of   , and for so doing this shall be your sufficient warrant; and that you also attend at the time and place above mentioned to make a return of the names of the persons whom you shall have so summoned and further to do and execute such other matters as shall be then and there enjoined you and have you then and there this warrant.

    Given under my hand and seal this   day of   , 19 .

Coroner.

FORM No. 3.

Declaration of Coroner that Inquest Necessary.

Province of Ontario,
    of
    To wit:

I,   of the   of in the   of   a Coroner in and for said   do hereby solemnly declare:

That after viewing the body of   (*or* the body of an unknown person) now lying dead at   , in this   , I am of opinion that there is good reason for believing that   (*or* an unknown man, woman *or* male *or* female child) now lyin   her) death from natural causes, or from mere accident or mischance; but came to his (*or* her) death from violent or unfair means, or culpable or negligent conduct of others, or under other circumstances requiring investigation by a Coroner's inquest.

And I make this solemn declaration conscientiously believing it to be true and knowing it is of the same force and effect as if made under oath and by virtue of *The Canada Evidence Act.*

Declared before me at the   of ⎤
    in the   of   , this ⎬
   day of   , 19   . ⎦

                              Coroner.

    A Commissioner, etc.

Form No. 4.

Warrant to Bury After a View.

Province of Ontario, ⎫ To the person in charge or
     of   ⎬ control of the burying
   To wit: ⎭ grounds in the and to all others whom it may concern.

Whereas, an inquisition hath this day been held upon view of the body of   , who now lies dead in your (township *or* city *or as the case may be*). These are therefore to certify that you may lawfully permit the body of the said   to be buried; and for your so doing this is your warrant

Given under my hand and seal this   day of   , 19   .

                              Coroner.

FORM No. 5.

Declaration of Coroner upon Order for Burial.

Province of Ontario, ⎫ In the matter of
        of ⎬   deceased.
    To wit: ⎭

I,   , Coroner of the   of   , in
the County of   , do solemnly declare that I
visited and examined the body of the said
and learned from   the following facts:—

Upon these facts I issued an order to bury the
body.

And I make this solemn declaration conscientiously believing it to be true, and knowing that it
is of the same force and effect as if made under oath
and by virtue of the Canada Evidence Act.

Declared before me at the   of ⎫
    in the   of   , this ⎬
day of   , 19 . ⎭
        A Commissioner, etc.

FORM No. 6.

Warrant to Medical Practitioner.

Province of Ontario, ⎫ To   , a legally quali-
        of ⎨ fied medical practitioner
    To wit: ⎬ of the   of   ,
        ⎭ in the   of   .

By virtue of my office these are in His Majesty's
name to charge and command you that you do
(ma   • nina-

tion of the body of   , now lying dead at the
     of   , in the County of   , without an
analysis, and) appear before me and my jury at
     , in the   of   , on the   day
of   , 19   , at   o'clock, and give further
evidence touching the death of   .

Given under my hand and seal this   day
of   , 19   .

Coroner.

The words between the brackets ( ) may be
omitted when a *post mortem* examination is not
required.

———

FORM No. 7.

Summons to a Juror.

Province of Ontario, ⎫
    of   ⎬
  To wit: ⎭

By virtue of a warrant under the hand and seal
of   , His Majesty's Coroner for this
of   of   , you are hereby summoned personally
to be and appear before him as a juryman on the
     day of   , at   o'clock,   in the
     precisely, at the   , known by the name
or sign of   , in the   of   , then and
there to enquire, on His Majesty's behalf, touching
the death of   , and further to do and execute
such other matters and things as shall be then and
there enjoined you, and not depart without leave.

Herein fail not at your peril.

Dated the   day of   , 19   .

To   , of   , in the   .

Constable.

FORM No. 8.

Summons to a Witness.

Province of Ontario, ⎫ To   , of the
        of   ⎬ of   , in the
    To wit: ⎭ of   .

Whereas I am credibly informed that you can give material evidence on behalf of our Sovereign Lord the King, touching the death of   , now lying dead in the   of   , in the said County of   . These are, therefore, by virtue of my office, in His Majesty's name, to charge and command you personally to be and appear before me at (*here insert a sufficient description of the place where the inquest is to be held*) in the said   at   of the clock in the   noon, on the   day of   , and then and there to give evidence and be examined, on His Majesty's behalf, before me and my inquest touching the premises.

Given under my hand and seal this   day of   , 19 .

                                    Coroner.

———

FORM No. 9.

Warrant to take up a Body Interred.

Province of Canada, ⎫ To the Minister and church-
    County of   ⎬ wardens of   (*or to*
        To wit: ⎭ *the proper authorities having charge of the place of burial*).

Whereas, complaint hath been made unto me, one   ·unty,

on the   day of   , that the body of one
was privately and secretly buried in your
township, and that the said   died, not of a
natural but violent death; and whereas no notice
of the violent death of the said   hath been
given to any of His Majesty's Coroners for the said
county, whereby, on IIis Majesty's behalf, an inquisition might have been taken on view of the
body of the said   before his interment, as by
law is required. These are, therefore, by virtue of
my office, in His Majesty's name, to charge and
command you that you forthwith cause the body of
the said   to be taken up and safely conveyed
to   in the said township, that I with my
inquest may have a view thereof, and proceed
therein according to law.

Herein fail not, as you will answer the contrary
at your peril.

Given under my hand and seal this   day
of   , one thousand nine hundred and   .

                                    Coroner, County of   .
                                              (L.S.)

FORM No. 10.

Warrant to Apprehend the Accused.

	To the constables of the
Province of Canada, County of	officers in the said county. other His Majesty's peace County of , and all Township of , in the

Whereas, by an inquisition taken before me,
          , one of His Majesty's Coroners for the said
county, this   day of   . at   , in
the said county, on view of the body of   then .

and there lying dead, one   , late of   ,
in the said county (*occupation*), stands charged with
the wilful murder of the said   . These are,
therefore, by virtue of my office, in His Majesty's
name, to charge and command you and every of
you, that you or some or one of you, without
delay, do apprehend and bring before me,   ,
the said Coroner, or one of His Majesty's justices of
the peace of the said county, the body of the said
          , of whom you shall have notice, that he may
be dealt with according to law; and for your so
doing this is your warrant.

    Given under my hand and seal this   day
of   , one thousand nine hundred and   ,

                      Coroner, County of   .

                            (L.S.)

FORM No. 11.

Warrant of Detainer.

Province of Canada, ⎱   To the keeper of His Ma-
   County of   ⎰   jesty's gaol at   , of
      To wit: the County of   ,

    Whereas you have in your custody the body of
          ; and whereas by an inquisition taken before
me, one of His Majesty's Coroners for the said
County of   ., the day and year hereunder
written, at the   of   in the said county,
on view of the body of   then and there lying
dead, he, the said   , stands charged with (*here
insert the crime charged, for instance,* the wilful
murder of the said   ).

    These are, therefore, in His Majesty's name, by
virtue of my office, to charge and command you
to   of the

said   , until he shall thence be discharged by due course of law; and for your so doing this is your warrant.

Given under my hand and seal this   day of   , one thousand nine hundred and   ,   ,

Coroner, County of   .

(L.S.)

FORM No. 12.

Information of Witnesses.

Dominion of Canada: ⎫
  Province of Ontario, ⎪
    County of ⎬
      To wit: ⎭

Information of witnesses severally taken and acknowledged on behalf of our Sovereign Lord the King touching the death of   at the known by the name or sign of   , in the of   , in the County of   , on the day of   , in the year of our Lord one thousand nine hundred and   , before me,   , one of His Majesty's Coroners for the said   , on an inquisition then and there taken, on view of the body of the said   , then and there lying dead, as follows, to wit: I   , of the   of   , in the said County of   , being sworn, saith:

FORM No. 13.

Exhibit No. ⎫
  Referred to by ⎬
    Dr. ⎭

REPORT OF THE POST MORTEM EXAMINATION made upon the body of   , about the age of

5

, at   , in the County of   , in the
Province of Ontario, on the   day of   ,
19 , about   hours after death.

Length of body.
Weight.
How nourished.

1. Peculiarities of—
     (a) Hair.
     (b) Teeth.
     (c) Eyes.
     (d) Scars, etc.
2. Rigor Mortis.
3. Post mortem staining.
4. Decomposition.
5. Marks of external violence.

INTERNAL EXAMINATION.

6. *Chest*—
     (a) Height of Diaphragm in Infants.
     (b) Pericardium.
7. *Heart*—Size and weight.
     (a) Right Auricle—contents.
     (b) Tricuspid Valve and Orifice.
     (c) Right Ventricle—contents.
     (d) Pulmonary Orifice and Valve.
     (e) Left Auricle—contents.
     (f) Mitral Orifice and Valve.
     (g) Left Ventricle—contents.
     (h) Aortic Orifice and Valve.
8. Aorta and Large Vessels.
9. Coronary Arteries.
10.

11. Mouth.
12. Tongue.
13. Aesophagus.
14. Larynx.
15. Trachea.
16. Bronchi.
17. Thyroid.
18. Thymus.
19. Pleurae—
    (a) Right.
    (b) Left.
20. Lungs—
    (a) Right.
    (b) Left.
21. *Abdomen*—Peritoneum, etc.
22. Stomach and contents.
23. Intestines and Mesenteric Glands.
24. Liver—
    (a) Surface.
    (b) Section.
    (c) Weight.
25. Gall Bladder.
26. Spleen.
27. Pancreas.
28. Kidneys and Ureters—
    (a) Right.
    (b) Left.
    (c) Suprarenal Bodies.
29. Bladder and contents.
30. Generative Organs—in the female—
    (a) Uterus.
    b Ovaries and Tubes.

31. *Head*—
    (*a*) Scalp.
    (*b*) Meninges and Blood Vessels.
32. Brain—
    (*a*) Hemisphere.
    (*b*) Ventricles.
    (*c*) Cornua.
    (*d*) Pons.
    (*e*) Cerebellum.
    (*f*) Medulla.
33. Spinal Cord.

———

FORM No. 14.

Warrant to Bring Prisoner from Gaol.

To the keeper of His Majesty's gaol at
in the County of   .

   Whereas you have in your custody the body of
   charged with the murder of   .

   These are by virtue of my office to command
you forthwith to deliver the said   into the
hands of the police officer,   , that the said
          may be present at my inquest now being
held upon the body of   .

   Herein fail not at your peril.

   Given under my hand and seal this   day
of   , 19   .

Coroner.

Form No. 15.

Dominion of Canada :
  Province of Ontario,
    County of
      To wit :

An inquisition indented taken for our Sovereign Lord the King, at the house of   , known by the sign of   , situate in the   of   , in the County of   , on the   day of   , in the *   year of the reign of our Sovereign Lord King George V., before   , Esquire, one of the said Coroners of our said Lord the King, for the said county, on view of the body of   , then and there lying dead, upon the oath of (*insert names of jurymen one below the other*) good and lawful men of the said county, duly chosen, and who being then and there duly sworn and charged to enquire for our Lord the King, when, where, how, and by what means the said   came to death, do upon their oath say : That

.

(*here insert verdict*)

In witness whereof, as well the said Coroner as the said jurors aforesaid have hereunto set and subscribed their hands and seals the day and year first above written. (*Coroner signs first, then the Foreman, then all the jury, one below the other.*)

*King George V ascended the Throne. May 6th. 1910.

FORM No. 16.

Recognizance Before Coroner.

Province of Ontario,

      Be it remembered, that
      and
      of the same place,
             do severally
acknowledge to owe to our Sovereign Lord the
King the sum of   Dollars each of lawful
money of Canada, to be levied on their several
goods and chattels, lands and tenements, by way of
recognizance, to His Majesty's use, in case default
shall happen to be made in the condition hereunder
written.

The condition of this recognizance is such, that
if the above bounden   and
do severally personally appear at the next general
gaol delivery to be holden in and for the county of
    , and the said   shall then and
there prefer, or cause to be preferred to the grand
jury, a bill of indictment against   late
of   and now in custody for the
of   late of   and that the said
and   do then and there severally
personally appear to give evidence upon such bill
of indictment to the said grand jury; and in case
the said bill of indictment be found by the grand
jury a true bill, that then the said   and
      do severally personally appear at the said
general gaol delivery, and the said   shall
then and there prosecute the said   on such
indictment, and the said   and   do
then and there severally give evidence to the jury
that shall pass on the trial of the said
touching the premises, and in case the said bill of
ind   t they

do severally personally appear at the said general gaol delivery, and then and there prosecute and give evidence to the jury that shall pass on the trial of the said   upon an inquisition taken before me, one of His Majesty's Coroners for the said   on view of the body of the said   , and not depart the Court without leave, then this recognizance to be void, otherwise to remain in full force.

Taken and acknowledge this   day of   , before me,

Coroner.

FORM No. 17.

Order for Payment of Jurors.

In the matter of the inquest upon
    I,   , an associate Coroner in and for the
        of   , do hereby certify that the persons whose names appear in the first column of the following schedule, who reside at the respective places named in the second column thereof, actually sat as jurors upon the inquest held by me as Coroner upon the body of   , deceased, on the
                day of   ,
A.D. 19 , and that the time occupied by such inquest was as follows:
and that the said jurors are entitled to mileage in the number of miles set opposite their names in the third column of the said schedule, and are respectively entitled to the sums set opposite their names in the fourth column of the said schedule, to compensate them for their fees and mileage pursuant to the Act fifty-ninth, Victoria, chapter 25, entitled

"An Act respecting the Fees of Jurors at Coroner's Inquests."

To the treasurer of the

Coroner.

SCHEDULE ABOVE REFERRED TO.

1 NAMES OF JURORS.	2 ADDRESS.	3 Mileage.	4 Amount Payable.	We, the undersigned, acknowledge receipt of the amounts payable to us at the date set opposite to our respective signatures.	Date of Payment.
1.					
2.					
3.					
4.					
5.					
6.					
7.					
8.					
9.					
10.					
11.					
12.					

Coroner.

FORM No. 18.

Certificate of Verdict.

County of   ,
To wit:

Inquest on the body of   held at   , in the County of   , on the   day of   , 19

Verdict: Murder against

FORM No. 19.

The Caption or Incipitur of a Fire Inquisition.

Province of Canada, }
County of
To wit: }

An inquisition indented, taken for our Sovereign Lord the King, at the house of , known by the sign of , situate in the of , in the County of , on the day of , in the year of the reign of our Sovereign Lord King George V., before , Esquire, one of the Coroners of our said Lord the King, for the said county, to inquire into the cause or origin of a certain fire which occurred in the said of , in the said year of the reign of our Sovereign George the V., at or about the hour of o'clock noon (*or* in the forenoon *or* afternoon *as the case may be*), whereby the house (*or other building*) of , situate upon lot number , on the side of street, in the said , (*or* upon lot number , in the concession of the Township of , in the said County of *as the case may be*), was wholly (*or* in part) consumed, upon the oath (*or* oath and affirmation) of (*naming all the jurors sworn*), good and lawful men of the said , duly chosen from among the householders resident in the vicinity of the said fire, and who being then and there duly sworn and charged to inquire for our said Lord the King, into the cause or origin of said fire, and whether it was kindled by design, or was the result of negligence or accident, do upon their oaths say, that, etc. (*then follows the verdict or finding of the jury, and after that the attestation or closing part of the inquisition, see Form No. 15, page 61*).

FORM No. 20.

By Hanging in Execution of Sentence of Death.

Canada:
Province of Ontario,
County of
    To wit:

[handwritten annotation]

An inquisition taken for our Sovereign Lord
the King, at the gaol or prison known by the
name of   , situate in the   of   ,
in the County of   , on the   day of
    , 19   , in the   year of the reign
of our Sovereign Lord George V., before   ,
Esquire, one of the Coroners of our said Lord
the King, for the said county, on view of the
body of   , then and there lying dead, upon
the oath (*or* oath and affirmation) of
(*naming all the jurors sworn*) good and lawful men
of the said county, duly chosen, and who being then
and there duly sworn, and charged to inquire for
our said Lord the King, when, where, how and by
what means the said   came to his death, do
upon their oath say: That the said   , being a
prisoner confined in the common gaol for the
County of   , under legal sentence that he be
hanged by the neck until he be dead, was, on
    day, the   day of   , A.D. 19   ,
within the walls of the said gaol, legally hanged
by the neck until he was dead, in pursuance and
in accordance with such sentence; and the jury
aforesaid, upon their oath aforesaid, do say, that
having enquired into the identity of the body, of
which they have had a view, and upon which this
inquest has been held, with that of the said prisoner
    , so under sentence of death as aforesaid,
th   ne, and

that judgment of death was duly executed upon the said offender. And the jurors aforesaid, upon their oath aforesaid, do further say, that the said   , in manner and by the means aforesaid, came to his death, and not otherwise.

In witness whereof, as well the said Coroner as the jurors aforesaid, have hereunto set and subscribed their hands and seals the day and year first above written.

Coroner signs first, then the Foreman of the jury, then the jury, one below another.

————

Form No. 21.

Caution to, and Statement of, the Accused.

Canada:
Province of Ontario,
    County of
        To wit:

A. B. stands charged before me, the undersigned, one of His Majesty's Coroners in and for the County of   , this   day of   , in the year of our Lord one thousand nine hundred and   , by an inquisition taken before me, this   day of   , in the year of our Lord one thousand nine hundred and   , at the of   , in the said County of   , on view of the body of   , then and there lying dead; for that the said   on the   day of   , in the year of our Lord one thousand nine hundred and   , at the   of   , in the County of   , did wilfully murder the said   (*or as the finding may be*), and the said charge being read to the said   , and the witnesses for the prosecution,   , being severally examined in his presence, the said   is now addressed by me as follows: "Having heard the evidence do you wish to say anything in answer to the charge? You are not bound to say anything, unless you desire to do so; but whatever you say will be taken down in writing, and may be given in evidence against you at your trial. You must clearly understand that you have nothing to hope from any promise of favour and nothing to fear from any threat which may have been held out to you to induce you to make any admission or confession of guilt, but whatever you now say may be given in evidence against you upon your trial, notwithstanding such promise or threat." Whereupon the said   saith as follows: (*here state whatever the prisoner may say, and in his very words as nearly as possible. Get him to sign it, if he will, at the end*).

Taken before me at   , the day and year first above mentioned.

J. S.,
Coroner, County of   .

...w your attention to an Amendment of
...e Coroners' Act." By Section 21,
...pter 17 of "The Ontario Statutes",
..., Item "D" of Schedule "A" of "The
...ners' Act" is amended so that it
...reads, as follows:

"...cessary travel, per mile 20 cents,
...when by railway, per mile 10 cents."

The Department of Audit of Crim-
...l Justice Accounts for Ontario has
...ded that this Amendment applies not
...y to cases of travel by the railroads,
...also to cities in which there are
...reet railways, and that, consequently,
...mileage allowance in the City of
...onto will, under the Amendment, be 10
...ts per mile.

This Amendment has been in force
...ce the Sixteenth day of April, 1912.

Yours truly,

Clerk of the Peace, County of

Form No. 22.

Form of Account to be rendered by the Coroner for the Collection of His Fees.

When an Inquest with a Jury was not Deemed Necessary.

The (*fill in City of*   , *or County of*   ,

as the case may be) to Dr.   , Coroner, Dr.

Date. 191		$	c.
	To fees on the body of .... Found dead at		
	To investigation into the cause of death, and declaration in writing, as required by 57 Vict. ch. 31, sec. 2, and 1 Geo. V. ch. 23	5	00
	To necessary travel from...... to ...... at 20c. a mile		

of   }

To wit: }

I   of the   of   , one of the Coroners in and for the County of   , make oath and say, that the above account is true, and the services were all rendered as charged therein.

Sworn before me at   of   ,   }
in the County of   . this   }
day of   . 191   .   }

FORM No. 23.

Form to be Used when an Inquest with a Jury has been held.

The *(fill in City of   , or County of   , as the case may be)* to Dr.   , Coroner, Dr.

(Fill i n D ates.) 191		$	c.
To fees on the body of			
Found dead at *(state where body was found)*			
Verdict of the jury, that the said			
Impanelling jury		2	00
Examination of each witness, including summons, 50 cents			
Taking each recognizance (50 cents)			
(If adjournments are made, give dates, number of witnesses and mileage for each.)			
Taking inquisition and making returns		10	00
Every warrant $1 each)			
(State what each warrant issued was for.)			
Order for payment of jurors..		1	00
Necessary travel from .... to ...... miles, at 20 cents per mile			
Total....			

Canada:
Province of Ontario,
County of
To wit:

I,   of the   , one of the Coroners in and for the   of   , make oath and say, that the above account is true, and the services were all rendered as charged therein.

Sworn before me at the   , of   ,
  in the   of , this   day of   ,
  in the year of our Lord 191 .

J.P.

(a) Warrant to constable to take possession, &c.
(b)   "   "   " to summon jury
(c)   "   " the dead man to make view
(d)   "   "   bury

FORM No. 24.

Fees Payable to Medical Man for Making Post Mortem Examination.

The City (*or* County) of   to Dr.   ,
Dr.

Date 191		$	c.
	To making a post mortem examination of the body of....		
	. . . .	15	00
	To .... miles travel from.... to .... and return at 20c. per mile		
	To attendance at inquest on body of ...... on a warrant signed by Dr. ....Coroner	5	00
	To .... miles travel from.... to .... and return at 20c per mile		
	Total	$	

The above was ordered and the services were duly rendered. The Treasurer will please pay.

                                   M.D.,
                                        Coroner.

Murder.

Copy caption as at page 61) that   , otherwise called   (*or, that a certain person to the
jurors aforesaid unknown*) on the   day of
     , in the year aforesaid, at   , in the
County of   , did feloniously, wilfully and of
his malice aforethought, kill and murder one   ,
against the peace of our Lord the King, his Crown
and dignity.

In witness, etc. (*finish with attestation as at
page 61*).

AIDERS AND ABETTORS.

Murder, Stating the Aid and Abetment Specially.

Copy caption as at page 61) that one
not having the fear of God before his eyes, but
being moved and seduced by the instigation of the
devil, on the   day of   in the year
aforesaid, the said   feloniously, wilfully and
of his malice aforethought did kill and murder (and
the jurors aforesaid, upon their oath aforesaid,
further say that   and   at the time of
the felony and murder aforesaid, to wit, on the
day and year aforesaid, were feloniously present
comforting, aiding, abetting and assisting the said
     the felony and murder aforesaid to do and
commit): and so the jurors aforesaid, upon their
oath aforesaid, do say, that the said   and
him, the said   , in manner aforesaid, feloniously, wilfully and of their malice aforethought, did
kill and murder, against the peace of our said Lord
the King, his Crown and dignity.

In witness, etc. (*finish with the attestation as at
page 61*).

6

ACCESSORIES BEFORE THE FACT.

*Murder, Charging the Accessories Jointly with the
Principal.*

*Copy caption as at page 61, and continue as in
the last precedent, omitting the charge within
brackets and then proceed)* and the jurors aforesaid, upon their oath aforesaid, further say, that
before the said felony and murder was committed, to wit, on the   day of   in the
year aforesaid, feloniously and maliciously did in-
cite, move, procure, aid, counsel, hire and command
the said   the said felony and murder to do
and commit, against the peace of our said Lord the
King, his Crown and dignity.

In witness, etc. *(copy attestation as at page 61).*

———

*Murder, Charging the Accessory Alone, Where the
Principal is Unknown.*

Copy caption as at page 61) that certain persons to the jurors aforesaid unknown, on the
day of   in the year aforesaid, feloniously,
wilfully and of their malice aforethought, the said
did kill and murder against the peace of our
said Lord the King, His Crown and dignity: and
the jurors aforesaid, upon their oath aforesaid, do
further say, that   before the said felony and
murder was committed, to wit, on the   day
of   in the year aforesaid, did feloniously and
maliciously counsel, hire, procure and command
the said persons to the said jurors aforesaid unknown as aforesaid, the said felony and murder to
do and commit against the peace of our said Lord
the King, his Crown and dignity.

ge 61).

Manslaughter.

Copy caption as at page 61) that   , on the   day of   , in the year aforesaid, at   , in the County of   , did feloniously and unlawfully kill and slay one   , against the peace of our Lord the King, his Crown and dignity.

In witness, etc. (*finish with attestation as at page 61*).

———

Homicide by Infants under Discretion.

By Drowning Himself.

Copy caption as at page 61, and then proceed) that the said   , then being an infant under the age of discretion, to wit, of the age of   years, not having discernment between good and evil, on the   day of   in the year aforesaid, into a certain river of water commonly called the   did cast and throw himself by means of which said casting and throwing the said   , then being such infant under the age of discretion as aforesaid, in the waters of the said river was then and there suffocated and drowned; of which said drowning and suffocation he, the said   , then and there instantly died: and so the jurors aforesaid upon their oath aforesaid, do say, that the said   , so being such infant under the age of discretion as aforesaid, in the manner and by the means aforesaid, did kill himself.

In witness, etc. (*finish with the attestation as at page 61).*

By Poisoning the Deceased.

Copy caption as at page 61) that one   ,
then being an infant and under the age of discretion, to wit, of the age of   years, not having
discernment between good and evil, on the
day of   in the year aforesaid, a large quantity of a certain deadly poison called   , to wit
(*quantity*) of the said   which the said
so being such infant as aforesaid, then accidentally
found, into and with a certain quantity of
did put, mix and mingle, the said   not knowing that the said   so as aforesaid by him
put, mixed and mingled into and with the said
was a deadly poison; and that the said
afterwards, to wit, on the day and year aforesaid,
did take, drink and swallow down a certain large
quantity, to wit (half a pint of the said fluid, with
which the said   was so mixed and mingled by
the said   , as aforesaid, the said   at the
time he so took, drank and swallowed down the said
, not knowing that there was any   or
any other poisonous or hurtful ingredient mixed or
mingled therewith; by means whereof he, the said
, then became sick and greatly distempered
in his body; and the said   , of the poison
aforesaid, so by him taken, drunk and swallowed
down as aforesaid and of the sickness occasioned
thereby, from the said   day of   in
the year aforesaid, until the   day of the same
month in the year aforesaid, did languish, and languishing did live; on which said last-mentioned day
in the year aforesaid he, the said   , of the
poison aforesaid and of the sickness and distemper
occasioned thereby, did die: and so the jurors aforesaid, upon their oath aforesaid, do say that the
said   , so being such infant under the age of
di   , in the

mȧnner and by the means aforesaid, did kill and slay, but not feloniously nor of his malice aforethought; and so the said   came to his death.

In witness, etc. (*finish with the attestation as at page 61*).

By Striking an Infant with a Hammer.

Copy caption as at page 61) that one   , then being an infant under the age of discretion, to wit, of the age of   years, not having discernment between good and evil, on the   day of   in the year aforesaid, with a certain hammer the said   , an infant of tender age, to wit, of the age of   years, in and upon the head of him the said   did strike, thereby then giving to the said   with the hammer aforesaid, in and upon the head of him the said   , one mortal bruise, of which said mortal bruise the said   , from the day and year last aforesaid, until the   day of   in the same year, did languish, and languishing did live, on which said last-mentioned day in the year aforesaid, the said   , of the said mortal bruise, did die: and so the jurors aforesaid, upon their oath aforesaid, do say, that the said   , so being such infant under the age of discretion as aforesaid, him, the said   , in the manner and by the means aforesaid, did kill and slay, but not feloniously nor of his malice aforethought; and so the said   came to his death.

In witness, etc. (*finish with the attestation as at page 61*).

Homicide by Madmen, Lunatics and Idiots.

By Shooting Himself.

Copy caption as at page 61) that the said
not being of sound mind, memory and understanding, but lunatic and distracted, on the
day of   in the year aforesaid, a certain pistol loaded and charged with gunpowder
and one leaden bullet, which pistol he, the said
, in his right hand then held, to and against
the head of him the said   , did shoot off and
discharge by means whereof the said   did
then give unto himself, with the leaden bullet aforesaid, so discharged and shot out of the pistol aforesaid, by force of the gunpowder aforesaid, in and
upon the head of him the said   one mortal
wound, of which said mortal wound he the said
then and there instantly died: and so the
jurors aforesaid, upon their oath aforesaid, do say,
that the said   not being of sound mind,
memory and understanding, but lunatic and distracted, in the manner and by the means aforesaid
did kill himself.

In witness, etc. *(finish with the attestation as at
page 61).*

By Cutting his Throat.

Copy caption as at page 61) that the said
not being of sound mind, memory and understanding, but lunatic and distracted, on the
day of   in the year aforesaid, with a
certain razor, which he, the said   , in his right
hand then held, the throat of him the said
did strike, stab and penetrate, thereby then giving
unto   afore-

said, in and upon the throat of him the said
one mortal wound, of which said mortal wound he
the said   then instantly died: and so the
jurors aforesaid, upon their oath aforesaid, do say,
that the said   , not being of sound mind,
memory and understanding, but lunatic and distracted, in the manner and by the means aforesaid,
did kill himself.

In witness, etc. (*finish with the attestation as at
page 61*).

By Hanging Himself.

Copy caption as at page 61) that the said
            not being of sound mind, memory and un-
derstanding, but lunatic and distracted, on the
            day of   in the year aforesaid, one end
of a certain piece of small cord unto an iron staple
then fastened into the ceiling of a certain room of
him the said   in the dwelling-house of one
            , situate at the   of   , in the
County of   , and the other end thereof about
his own neck did fix, tie and fasten, and therewith
then did hang, suffiocate and strangle himself, of
which said hanging, suffocation and strangling he
the said   then instantly died: and so the
jurors aforesaid, upon their oath aforesaid, do say,
that the said   not being of sound mind,
memory and understanding, but lunatic and distracted, in the manner and by the means aforesaid,
did kill himself.

In witness, etc. (*finish with the attestation as at
page 61*).

By Poisoning Himself.

Copy caption as at page 61) that the said
            not being of sound mind, memory and un-

derstanding, but lunatic and distracted, on the day of   in the year aforesaid, a certain large quantity of a certain deadly poison called   , to wit, (*quantity*), of the said   , into a certain quantity of   did put, mix and mingle, and a large quantity of the said fluid, to wit, half a pint of the said fluid, with which the said   was so then put, mixed and mingled as aforesaid, the said   , not being of sound mind, memory and understanding, but lunatic and distracted as aforesaid, did then take, drink and swallow down, by means whereof the said   then became sick and distempered in his body, and of the poison aforesaid so by him taken, drunk and swallowed down as aforesaid, and of the sickness and distemper occasioned thereby, from the said   day of   in the year aforesaid, until the   day of the same month of   in the year aforesaid, did languish and languishing did live, on which said last mentioned day in the year aforesaid, he the said   of the poison aforesaid, and of the sickness and distemper occasioned thereby, did die: and so the jurors aforesaid, on their oath aforesaid, do say, that the said   , not being of sound mind, memory and understanding, but lunatic and distracted, in the manner and by the means aforesaid, did kill himself.

In witness, etc. (*finish with the attestation as at page 61*).

———

By Drowning Himself.

(*Copy caption as at page 61*) that the said   not being of sound mind, memory and understanding, but lunatic and distracted, on the day of   in the year aforesaid, into a cert   of

, in the County of   , did cast and throw himself, by means of which said casting and throwing he, the said   , not being of sound mind, memory and understanding, but lunatic and distracted, in the waters of the said pond was then suffocated and drowned, of which said drowning and suffocation he, the said   , then instantly died: and so the jurors aforesaid, upon their oath aforesaid, do say, that the said   not being of sound mind, memory and understanding, but lunatic and distracted, in the manner and by the means aforesaid, did kill himself.

In witness, etc. (*finish with the attestation as at page 61*).

———

By Throwing Himself out of a Window.

Copy caption as at page 61) that the said   not being of sound mind, memory and understanding, but lunatic and distracted, on the   day of   in the year aforesaid, from and out of a certain window in the dwelling-house of him the said   , situate at the   of   , in the County of   , did violently cast and throw himself to the ground, to and against a certain stone pavement then there being, by means of which said casting and throwing to and against the said stone pavement, he, the said   , did then receive one mortal wound on the upper part of the head of him, the said   , of which said mortal wound he, the said   , then instantly died: and so the jurors aforesaid, upon their oath aforesaid, do say, that the said   , in the manner and by the means aforesaid, not being of sound mind, memory and understanding, but lunatic and distracted, did kill himself.

In witness, etc. (*finish with the attestation as at page 61*).

By Throwing the Deceased out of a Window.

Copy caption as at page 61) that one   ,
not being of sound mind, memory and understanding, but lunatic and distracted, on the   day
of   in the year aforesaid, him the said
through and out of a certain window of a certain
dwelling-house, situate at the   of   , in
the County of   , to and against the ground
then did violently cast and throw, thereby giving
to the said   , by the casting and throwing aforesaid, to and against the ground as aforesaid, a violent concussion of the brain, of which said violent
concussion the said   then instantly died: and
so the jurors aforesaid, upon their oath aforesaid,
do say, that the said   , not being of sound
mind, memory and understanding, but lunatic and
distracted, him, the said   , in manner and by
the means aforesaid, did kill and slay, but not
feloniously nor of his malice aforethought, and so
the said   came to his death.

In witness, etc. *(finish with the attestation as at
page 61)*.

Homicide in a Fit of Delirium.

By Shooting Himself.

Copy caption as at page 61) that the said
       , then labouring under a grievous disease of
the body, to wit, a fever *(or as the case may be)*
and by reason of the violence of the said grievous
disease, then being delirious and out of his mind, on
the   day of   in the year aforesaid, a
certain pistol loaded with gunpowder and one
leaden bullet, which said pistol the said   in
his   head

of him, the said   , he, the said   , being
so delirious and out of his mind as aforesaid, did
shoot off and discharge, thereby then giving unto
himself in and upon the head of him, the said
, with the leaden bullet aforesaid out of the
pistol aforesaid, then by force of the gunpowder
aforesaid shot off and discharged as aforesaid, one
mortal wound, of which said mortal wound he, the
said   , then instantly died: and so the jurors
aforesaid, upon their oath aforesaid, do say, that
the said   so being delirious and out of his
mind as aforesaid, in the manner and by the means
aforesaid, did kill himself.

In witness, etc. (*finish with the attestation as at
page 61*).

Killed by Explosion of Boiler of Steam Engine.

Copy caption as at page 61) that on the
day of   , in the year aforesaid, the said
being on board of a certain steamboat called the
, then floating and being navigated on the
water of the river,   it so happened that accidentally, casually and by misfortune a certain
boiler containing water, and then forming part of
a certain steam engine in and on board of the said
steamboat and attached thereto, and which said
boiler was then used and employed in the working
of the said steam engine, for the purpose of pro-
pelling the said steamboat along the said river, and
was then heated by means of a fire, then also forming part of the said steam engine in the said steamboat, burst and exploded, by means whereof a large
quantity, to wit, ten gallons of the boiling and
scalding water and steam then being within the
cavity of the said boiler, and a large quantity, to
wit, one bushel of hot and burning cinders and

coals forming part of the said fire, accidentally, casually and by misfortune were cast, thrown and came from and out of the said boiler and steam engine with great force and violence upon and against the head, face and neck of him, the said   , whereby he, the said   , then received in and upon his head, face and neck divers mortal burns and scalds, of which said mortal burns and scalds, he the said   , then instantly died: and so the jurors aforesaid, upon their oath aforesaid, do say, that the said   , in manner and by the means aforesaid, accidentally, casually and by misfortune came to his death, and not otherwise.

In witness, etc. (*finish with attestation as at page 61*).

———

Killed by Collision on a Railway.

Copy caption as at page 61) that on the   day of   , in the year aforesaid, a certain locomotive steam-engine, numbered   , with a certain tender attached thereto and worked therewith, and also with divers, to wit, ten carriages used for the conveyance of passengers for hire, on a certain railway called the   Railway, and which said carriages respectively were then attached and fastened together and to the said tender, and were then propelled by the said locomotive steam-engine, were moving and travelling along the said railway towards the Town of   . And the jurors aforesaid, upon their oaths aforesaid, do further say, that whilst and during the time the said locomotive steam-engine, tender and carriages were so moving and travelling along the said railway as aforesaid, a certain other locomotive steam-engine, numbered   , with a certain other tender attached   1 also with divers, to wit, five other carriages, used for the conveyance of passengers for hire, on the said railway, and which said last mentioned carriages respectively, were then attached and fastened together and to the said last mentioned tender, and were then propelled by the said last mentioned locomotive steam-engine, and in one of which said last mentioned carriages the said   was then a passenger, and was then riding and being carried and conveyed therein, were then also moving and travelling along the said railway in a direction from the said Town of   , and towards the said first mentioned locomotive steam-engine, tender and carriages; and that the said first mentioned locomotive steam-engine, tender and carriages, and the said secondly mentioned locomotive steam-engine, tender and carriages being then so respectively moving and travelling upon the said railway in different and opposite directions as aforesaid, then accidentally, casually and by misfortune, came into sudden, violent and forcible contact and collision; by means whereof the said   then received divers mortal wounds, bruises and concussions; of which said mortal wounds, bruises and concussions he, the said   , then instantly died. And so the jurors aforesaid, upon their oaths aforesaid, do say that the said   , in manner and by the means aforesaid, accidentally, casually and by misfortune, came to his death, and not otherwise.

In witness, etc. (*finish with attestation as at page 61*).

———

Excusable Homicide.

By Shooting at Butts.

Copy caption as at page 61) that   , on the   day of   , in the year aforesaid, a

certain gun charged with gunpowder and a leaden
bullet, which he, the said   , then had and
held in both his hands, casually and by misfortune,
and against the will of him,, the said   , was
discharged and shot off; and that the said   ,
with the leaden bullet aforesaid, then discharged
and shot out of the said gun by the force of the
gunpowder aforesaid, him, the said   , in and
upon the left breast of him, the said   , casually, by misfortune, and against the will of him,
the said   , did then strike and penetrate,
thereby then giving unto him, the said   , with
the bullet aforesaid, out of the gun aforesaid, so
shot off and discharged as aforesaid, in and upon the
said left breast of him, the said   , one mortal
wound, of which said mortal wound he, the said
        , then instantly died. And so the jurors, etc.
(*conclude as in the above precedent, and with the
attestation as at page 61*).

By a Knife.

Copy caption as at page 61) that the said
and one   , on the   day of   , in the
year aforesaid, being infants under the age of
twelve years, in the peace of God, and of our said
Lord the King, then being in friendship, and wan-
tonly and in play struggling together, and then
and there both falling to the ground, it so happened
that, casually and by misfortune, and against the
will of him, the said   , the said   then
fell upon the point of a certain open clasp knife,
which he, the said   , then had and held in his
right hand; by means of which said falling he, the
said   , did then, casually, by misfortune, and
agai   re one

mortal wound in and upon the right breast of him, the said   , of the breadth of one inch, and depth of three inches; of which said mortal wound the said   , from the said   day of   , in the year aforesaid, until the   day of   , in the same year, did languish, and languishing did live; on which said   day of   , in the year aforesaid, the said   of the mortal wound aforesaid did die. And so the jurors, etc. (*conclude as on page 85*).

In Defence of Person.

Copy caption as at page 61) that on the day of   , in the year aforesaid, the said   being in a certain common drinking-room belonging to a public house, known by the sign of   , in which said common drinking-room one   and divers other persons were then present, the said   , without any cause or provocation whatsoever given by the said   , did then menace and threaten the said   to turn him, the said   , out of the said common drinking-room, and for that purpose did then lay hold of the person of him, the said   , and on him, the said   , violently did make an assault, and him, the said   , without any cause or provocation whatsoever did then beat, abuse and ill-treat; whereupon the said   , for the preservation and safety of his person, and of inevitable necessity, did then, with the hands of him, the said   , defend himself against such the violent assault of him, the said   , as it was lawful for him to do; and the said   did then receive, against the will of him, the said   , by the falls and blows which he, the said   , then sustained by his, the said   's so defending

himself as aforesaid, divers mortal bruises in and
upon the head, back and loins of him, the said   ;
of which said mortal bruises he, the said   ,
from the said   day of   , in the year
aforesaid, until the   day of the same month in
the same year did languish, and languishing did
live; on which said   day of   ,in the
year aforesaid, the said   of the mortal bruises
aforesaid did die.   And so the jurors aforesaid,
upon their oath aforesaid, do say that the said
him the said   , in the defence of himself, the
said   , in manner and by the means aforesaid,
did kill and slay.

In witness, etc. (*finish with attestation as at
page 61*).

Justifiable Homicide.

Against a Street Robber.

(*Copy caption as at page 61*) that the said
, with certain other persons to the jurors
aforesaid unknown, on the   day of   ,
in the year aforesaid, in and upon   , in the
King's highway then being, feloniously did make
an assault, and him, the said   , in bodily fear
and danger of his life did then put, and one gold
watch of the goods and chattels of him, the said
, from the person and against the will of him,
the said   , in the King's highway aforesaid
then feloniously did steal, take and carry away,
against the peace of our said Lord the King, his
Crown and dignity.   And the jurors aforesaid,
upon their oath aforesaid, do say that after the
said   and the said persons to the jurors
aforesaid unknown, had done and committed the
felc

and the said persons to the jurors aforesaid unknown, did then endeavour to fly and escape for
the same; whereupon the said   , together with
    and   and certain other persons to the
jurors aforesaid unknown, called in and taken to
their assistance, did then pursue and endeavour to
take and apprehend the said   and the said
persons to the jurors aforesaid unknown, for the
doing and the committing of the said felony and
robbery; and that the said   in such pursuit
was overtaken by them the said   and   and
the said persons to the jurors aforesaid unknown:
whereupon the said   and the said persons
to the jurors aforesaid unknown, did then lawfully
and peaceably endeavour to take and apprehend
the said   , who was then peaceably required
to surrender himself, in order to be brought to justice for the felony and robbery aforesaid; and that
the said   , to prevent his being taken and
apprehended, did then with a pistol loaded with
gunpowder and a leaden bullet which he, the said
    , then had and held in his right hand, menace
and threaten to shoot the first man that should
attempt to seize him, the said   ; and that the
said   did then refuse to surrender himself,
and did obstinately and unlawfully stand upon his
defence, in open defiance of the laws of this province; and that upon such endeavour to take and
apprehend the said   , he, the said   ,
did then discharge and shoot off the said pistol so
loaded with gunpowder and a leaden bullet as
aforesaid, at and against him, the said   ; and
that on the said   so continuing obstinately
and unlawfully to resist and refuse to surrender
himself to public justice, they, the said   and
    , in order to apprehend and take the said
    , to be brought to justice for the said felony

7

and robbery, and in order to oblige the said
to surrender himself for the purposes aforesaid,
did then, justifiably and of inevitable necessity,
attack and assault the said   , by means whereof the said   did then receive in such his
obstinate and unlawful defence, and before he
could be taken and apprehended, divers mortal
wounds and bruises, of which said mortal wounds
and bruises the said   did languish,
and languishing did live; and that after the said
          was so wounded and bruised as aforesaid,
he, the said   , was then taken and apprehended, and on the day and year last mentioned
was lawfully committed to the common gaol for the
County of   , and of such mortal wounds and
bruises did then and there languish, and languishing did live; on which said day of   in the
year aforesaid, within the gaol aforesaid, the said
          of the mortal wounds and bruises aforesaid
did die. And so the jurors aforesaid, upon their
oath aforesaid, do say that the said   and
          , him, the said   , in manner and by
means aforesaid, in the pursuit of justice, of inevitable necessity and justifiably, did kill and slay.

In witness (*finish with attestation as at page
61*).

––––––

Accidental Death.

Crushed by a Cart.

(*Copy caption as at page 61*) that   on the
          day of   , in the year aforesaid, in a
certain public highway in the   of   , in
the county aforesaid, being driving a certain cart
drawn by three horses, and laden with twelve sacks
of coal, it so happened that the said   being
in   ·ntally,

casually and by misfortune forced to the ground
by the foremost horse of the said three horses so
drawing the said cart, and the said cart so laden as
aforesaid, was then there by the said horses violently and forcibly drawn to and against the said
, and the off-wheel of the said cart so drawn
and laden as aforesaid, did then there accidentally,
casually and by misfortune violently go upon and
pass over the breast and body of the said , by
means whereof the said from the weight
and pressure of the said cart, so laden and drawn
as aforesaid, did then receive one mortal bruise in
and upon his said breast and body, of which said
mortal bruise the said then instantly died:
and so the jurors aforesaid, upon their oath aforesaid, do say, that the said , in manner and by
the means aforesaid, accidentally, casually and by
misfortune came to his death, and not otherwise.

In witness, etc. (*finish with attestation as at
page 61*).

By Falling from a Cart.

Copy caption as at page 61) that the said ,
on the day of , in the year aforesaid,
being in company with certain boys to the jurors
aforesaid unknown, and a scavenger's empty cart
then standing on the top of a hill, they agreed together to get into the said empty cart, and afterwards to run and force the same down the said
hill, and that in the forcing and running of the
said cart down the said hill, and the said
then being in the said cart, it so happened that
accidentally, casually and by misfortune the said
cart, by reason of the violence of its being forced
down the said hill, overturned, and the said
was then thrown out of the said cart to and upon

the ground, under the head-board of the said cart, by means whereof the pulmonary vessels of him, the said   , were then broken, and the said   then also received divers mortal bruises in and upon the breast of him, the said   , of which said mortal bruises, and also by the breaking of the pulmonary vessels aforesaid, the said   then and there instantly died: and so the jurors aforesaid, upon their oath aforesaid, do say, that the said   , in the manner and by the means aforesaid. accidentally, casually and by misfortune came to his death, and not otherwise.

In witness, etc. (*finish with attestation as at page 61*).

———

Drowned by the Overturning of a Boat.

Copy caption as at page 61) that the said   , on the   day of   , in the year aforesaid, being ordered by one   , his master, to fasten the boat of the said   to her moorings or road in the river   instead thereof did then pin the same to a pile, under one of the arches of   , and in the said boat the said   did then lay himself down to sleep. and it so happened that by the flowing in of the tide the said boat (the said   being then asleep in the same) was then forced athwart the said arch, and pinned down and overset. by means whereof the said   was then accidentally, casually and by misfortune thrown out of the said boat into the said river   and in the waters thereof was then suffocated and drowned, of which said suffocation and drowning the said   then instantly died: and so the jurors aforesaid, upon their oath aforesaid, do say, th   by the means aforesaid, came to his death, and not otherwise.

In witness, etc. (*finish with attestation as at page 61*).

———

By the Fright of a Horse.

Copy caption as at page 61) that the said   ,
on the   day of   , in the year aforesaid,
then riding and galloping on a certain gelding, on a
certain highway in the   of   , in the
county aforesaid, it so happened that the said
gelding took fright at a certain cow which then
suddenly appeared and crossed the said highway
wherein the said   was then riding the said
gelding, and that the said gelding fell over the said
cow, and accidentally, casually and by misfortune
then flung the said　.,   with great violence to
and against the ground there, by means whereof
the said   .   then received one mortal fracture
on the upper part of the head of him, the said
          , of which said mortal fracture the said
then instantly died: and so the jurors aforesaid,
upon their oath aforesaid, do say, that the said
          in manner and by the means aforesaid, accidentally, casually and by misfortune came to his
death, and not otherwise.

In witness, etc. (*finish with attestation as at page 61*).

———

By the Kick of a Horse.

Copy caption as at page 61) that the said   ,
on the   day of   , in the year aforesaid,
was riding upon a certain horse of   , Esquire,
and the said   from the back of the said

horse then casually fell to the ground, and the horse aforesaid then struck the said   with one of his hinder feet, and thereby then gave to the said   upon the head of the said   one mortal wound, of which the said   did languish and languishing did live, from the said   day of   , in the year aforesaid, until the   day of   , in the year aforesaid, on which said   day of   , in the year aforesaid, the said   , of the mortal wound aforesaid, died: and so the jurors aforesaid, upon their oath aforesaid, do say, that the said   , in manner and form aforesaid, and not otherwise, came to his death.

In witness, etc (*finish with attestation as at page 61*).

By Falling from a Hay-loft, being in Liquor.

Copy caption as at page 61) that the said   , on the   day of   , in the year aforesaid, being in a certain hay-loft, in the stable yard of   , situate in the township of   , in the county aforesaid, and then being greatly intoxicated and in liquor, it so happened that, accidentally, casually, and by misfortune, the said   fell out of the said hay-loft to and against the ground there (which said ground was then paved with bricks); by means of which said fall the said   then received a violent concussion of the brain; of which said violent concussion the said   from the said   day of   , in the year aforesaid, until the   day of the same month, in the same year, did languish, and languishing did live; on which said   day of   , in the year aforesaid, the said   , of the   nd so the jurors aforesaid, upon their oath aforesaid, do say, that the said   in manner and by the means aforesaid, accidentally, casually and by misfortune came to his death, and not otherwise.

In witness, etc. (*finish with attestation as at page 61*).

————

Drowned.

Copy caption as at page 61) that the said   , on the   day of   , in the year aforesaid, being employed by   to carry and wheel gravel in a certain wheel-barrow, over a certain long and narrow plank of wood, braced with cords unto two wooden poles, lying over a certain deep pond of water, situate at the   of   , in the county aforesaid, it so happened that the said   , in wheeling the said wheel-barrow, so filled with the said gravel, over the said plank, accidentally, casually and by misfortune, fell from the said plank into the said pond, and in the waters thereof was then suffocated and drowned; of which said suffocation and drowning the said   then instantly died. And so the jurors aforesaid, upon their oath aforesaid, do say that the said   , in manner and by the means aforesaid, accidentally, casually and by misfortune, came to his death, and not otherwise.

In witness, etc. (*finish with attestation as at page 61*).

————

Drowned by Bathing.

Copy caption as at page 61) that the said   , on the   day of   , in the year aforesaid, going into a certain pond situate in the   of

, in the county aforesaid, to bathe, it so happened that accidentally, casually and by misfortune, the said   was in the waters of the said pond then suffocated and drowned, of which said suffocation and drowning the said   then instantly died: and so the jurors aforesaid, upon their oath aforesaid, do say, that the said
in manner and by the means aforesaid, accidentally, casually and by misfortune came to his death, and not otherwise.

In witness, etc. (*finish with attestation as at page 61*).

———

Drowned by Falling out of a Boat.

Copy caption as at page 61) that the said   , on the   day of   , in the year aforesaid, being with other children in a certain lighter commonly called a ballast-lighter, then floating in a certain deep pond of water, situate at the   of   , in the county aforesaid, it so happened that the said   accidentally, casually and by misfortune, fell from the said lighter into the said pond, and in the waters thereof was then suffocated and drowned, of which said suffocation and drowning, the said   then instantly died: and so the jurors aforesaid, upon their oath aforesaid, do say that the said   in manner and by the means aforesaid, accidentally, casually and by misfortune came to his death, and not otherwise.

In witness, etc. (*finish with attestation as at page 61*).

———

Found Drowned.

Copy caption as at page 61) that the said man to t

day of   , in the year aforesaid, was found
drowned and suffocated in a certain pond situated
at the   of   , in the county aforesaid,
and that the said man to the jurors aforesaid unknown, had no marks of violence appearing on his
body, but how or by what means the said man became drowned and suffocated, no evidence doth
appear to the jurors.

In witness, etc. (*finish with attestation as at
page 61*).

————

By a Fire.

Copy caption as at page 61) that on the
day of   , in the year aforesaid, the warehouse
of   , situate at the   of   , in the
county aforesaid, casually took fire, and the said
          , being then present, and aiding and assist-
ing to extinguish the said fire, it so happened that
a piece of timber, by the force and violence of the
said fire, accidentally, casually, and by misfortune,
fell from the top of the said warehouse upon the
head of him, the said   , by means whereof the
said   then received one mortal fracture on
the head of him, the said   , of which said
mortal fracture, the said   from the
day of   , in the year aforesaid, until the
          day of the same month, in the same year,
did languish and languishing did live; on which
said   day of   , in the year aforesaid, the
said   of the said mortal fracture did die:
and so the jurors aforesaid, upon their oath aforesaid do say, that the said   in manner and
by the means aforesaid, accidentally, casually and
by misfortune came to his death, and not otherwise.

In witness, etc. (*finish with attestation as at
page 61*).

By Being Burnt.

Copy caption as at page 61) that the said   ,
on the   day of   , in the year aforesaid,
being alone in her room or apartment, in a certain
almshouse, situate at the   of   , in the
county aforesaid, it so happened as she, the said
    , was then there sitting by her fireside, that
the woollen petticoat of her, the said   , which
she, the said   , then had on her body, accidentally, casually and by misfortune took fire, by
means whereof, and from the smoke and flame arising from the said fire, the said   was then
suffocated and burnt, of which said suffocation and
burning the said   then instantly died: and
so the jurors aforesaid, upon their oath aforesaid,
do say that the said   , in manner and by the
means aforesaid, accidentally, casually and by misfortune came to her death, and not otherwise.

In witness, etc. (*finish with attestation as at
page 61*).

By Being Suffocated.

Copy caption as at page 61) that the said   ,
on the   day of   , in the year aforesaid,
being intoxicated with liquor, and laying himself
down to sleep near unto a certain tile kiln then
burning in a certain field, commonly called the
brick field, situate at the   of   , in
the county aforesaid, it so happened that accidentally, casually and by misfortune, the said
by the smoke and sulphurous smell arising from
the fire in the said tile kiln, was there and then
choked, suffocated and stifled, of which said choking,
suffocation and stifling the said   then instantly
died :   oath

and by the means aforesaid, accidentally, casually and by misfortune came to his death, and not otherwise.

In witness, etc. (*finish with attestation as at page 61*).

Suffocated in the Mud.

Copy caption as at page 61) that the said   , on the   day of   , in the year aforesaid, being on board a certain ship or vessel, called the *Fortune*, of Leith, then lying at her moorings near the Hermitage, in the river Thames, in the   of   , in the county aforesaid, it so happened that the said   accidentally, casually and by misfortune fell from the side of the said ship or vessel into the mud or soil then being in the said river, by means whereof the said in the mud or soil of the said river was then suffocated and smothered, of which said suffocation and smothering the said   then instantly died: and so the jurors aforesaid, upon their oath aforesaid, do say, that the said   , in manner and by the means aforesaid, accidentally, casually and by misfortune came to his death, and not otherwise.

In witness, etc. (*finish with attestation as at page 61*).

Of a Child by Sudden Delivery.

Copy caption as at page 61) that   , the mother of the said new-born male child, on the   day of   , in the year aforesaid, the said male child did bring forth of her body alive suddenly and by surprise, and that the said new-born male child then died soon after its birth, in a natural way, and not from any violence, hurt or injury received from the said   , its mother, or any other person, to the knowledge of the said jurors; nor had the said new-born male child any marks of violence appearing on his body.

In witness, etc. (*finish with attestation as at page 61*).

———

By a Difficult Birth and Hard Labour.

Copy caption as at page 61) that the said   , on the   day of   , in the year aforesaid, being big with a certain female child, afterwards, to wit, on the same day and year, after a violent and lingering pain and hard labour, with great difficulty did bring forth the said female child alive; and that the said   , from the said   day of   , in the year aforesaid, until the   day of the same month, in the same year, of the weakness and disorder occasioned by such violent and lingering pain, difficult birth and hard labour aforesaid, did languish and languishing did live; on which said   day of   , in the year aforesaid, the said   of the weakness and disorder aforesaid, occasioned by the hard labour and difficult birth aforesaid, did die: and so the jurors aforesaid, upon their oath aforesaid, do say that the said   , in manner and by the means aforesaid, came to her death, and not otherwise.

In witness, etc. (*finish with attestation as at page 61*).

———

Still-Born.

Copy caption as at page 61) that the said new-born female child was still-born.

In witness, etc. (*finish with attestation as at page

Suicide.

By Hanging Himself.

Copy caption as at page 61) that the said ,
not having the fear of God before his eyes, but
being moved and seduced by the instigation of the
devil, on the   day of   in the year aforesaid, in and upon himself in the peace of God, and
of our said Lord the King then being, feloniously,
wilfully and of his malice aforethought, did make
an assault; and that the said   one end of a
certain piece of small cord unto a certain iron bar
then fixed in the ceiling of His Majesty's gaol for
the County of   (wherein the said   was
then a prisoner in custody charged with felony) and
the other end thereof about his own neck did then
fix, tie and fasten, and therewith did then hang,
suffocate and strangle himself, of which said hanging, suffocation and strangling he, the said   ,
then instantly died: and so the jurors aforesaid,
upon their oath aforesaid, do say, that the said
, in the manner and by the means aforesaid,
feloniously, wilfully and of his malice aforethought,
did kill and murder himself, against the peace of
our said Lord the King, his Crown and dignity; and
that the said   at the time of committing the
felony and murder aforesaid had no goods or chattels, lands or tenements within the said county or
elsewhere, to the knowledge of the said jurors.

In witness, etc. (*finish with the attestation as at
page 61*).

By Stabbing Himself.

*Copy caption as at page 61 and then continue
as in the preceding form*) did make an assault; and

that the said   with a certain drawn sword,
which he, the said   , in his right hand then
had and held, did then give unto himself one mortal wound upon the belly of him, the said   ,
under his left breast, of the breadth of one inch,
and of the depth of six inches, of which said mortal
wound he, the said   , then instantly died : and
so the jurors aforesaid, upon their oath aforesaid,
do say, that the said   , in the manner and by the
means aforesaid, feloniously, wilfully and of his
malice aforethought, did kill and murder himself
against the peace of our said Lord the King, his
Crown and dignity; (and that the said   , at
the time of the said felony and murder, so as aforesaid done and committed, had no goods or chattels,
lands or tenements, within the said county or elsewhere, to the knowledge of the said jurors).

In witness, etc. (*finish with the attestation as at
page 61*).

By Shooting Himself.

*Copy caption as at page 61, and then continue
as at page 101*) did make an assault; and that
the said   a certain pistol charged with gunpowder and one leaden bullet, which he, the said
          , in his right hand then had and held, feloni-
ously, wilfully and of his malice aforethought, to
and against the head of him, the said   , did
then shoot off and discharge ; and that the said
with the leaden bullet aforesaid, out of the pistol
aforesaid, then by force of the gunpowder aforesaid shot and sent forth as aforesaid, in and upon
the head of him, the said   , feloniously, wilfully
and of his malice aforethought, did strike, wound
and penetrate, then giving unto himself with the
leade   irged

and shot out of the pistol aforesaid by the force of
the gunpowder aforesaid, in and upon the head of
him, the said   , one mortal wound, of the breadth
of one inch and depth of three inches, of which said
mortal wound he, the said   , then instantly died:
and so the jurors, etc. (*conclude as in form on
page 85*).

By Drowning Himself.

Commence as in form on page 61) did make an
assault, and that the said   into a certain pond
there situate, wherein there was a great quantity of
water. then and there feloniously, wilfully and of
his malice aforethought, did cast and throw himself;
by means of which said casting and throwing into
the pond aforesaid, he, the said   in the pond
aforesaid with the water aforesaid was then and
there choked, suffocated and drowned; of which
said choking, suffocation and drowning he, the said
      , then and there instantly died. And so the
jurors, etc. (*conclude as in form on page 85*).

By Poisoning Himself.

Copy caption as at page 61) that the said
      not having the fear of God before his eyes,
but being moved and seduced by the instigation of
the devil, and of his malice aforethought, wickedly
contriving and intending with poison wickedly, feloniously and of his malice aforethought to kill and
murder himself, on the   day of   , in the
year aforesaid, feloniously, wilfully and of his
malice aforethought a large quantity of a certain
deadly poison called   . to wit,   , into

and with a certain quantity of   , feloniously, wilfully and of his malice aforethought, did put, mix and mingle, the said   then well knowing the said   so as aforesaid by him put, mixed and mingled with the said   as aforesaid, to be a deadly poison; and the said   a large quantity, to wit,   in which the said   was so put, mixed and mingled by the said   as aforesaid, afterwards, to wit, on the day and year aforesaid, feloniously, wilfully and of his malice aforethought, did take, drink and swallow down, by means whereof he, the said   , then became sick and greatly distempered in his body, and of the poison aforesaid, and of the sickness and distemper occasioned thereby, from the said   day of   in the year aforesaid, until the   day of the same month in the same year, did languish, and languishing did live, on which said last mentioned day, in the year aforesaid, he, the said   , of the poison, sickness and distemper aforesaid did die. And so the jurors, etc. (*conclude as on page 85*).

––––

By Strangling Himself.

Copy caption as at page 61, and continue as at page 101, and then proceed thus) did make an assault; and that the said   a certain silk handkerchief about the neck of him, the said   , then and there feloniously, wilfully and of his malice aforethought, did fix, tie and fasten; and that the said   with the silk handkerchief aforesaid, then feloniously, wilfully, and of his malice aforethought, did choke, suffocate and strangle himself, of which said choking, suffocation and strangling he, the said   , then instantly died. And so the jurors, etc. (*finish as on page 61*)

By Cutting his Throat.

Copy caption as at page 61 and continue as at page 101, and then proceed thus) did make an assault; and that the said   , with a certain razor, which he, the said   in his right hand then had and held, the throat of him, the said   , did then strike and cut, thereby then giving unto himself with the razor aforesaid, in and upon the throat of him, the said   , one mortal wound of the length of three inches, and of the depth of one inch; of which said mortal wound he, the said   , then instantly died; and so the jurors aforesaid, upon their oath aforesaid, do say, that the said in manner and by the means aforesaid feloniously, wilfully and of his malice aforethought, did kill and murder himself, against the peace of our said Lord the King, his Crown and dignity.

In witness whereof, etc. (*finish with attestation as at page 61*).

Starved.

Copy caption as at page 61) that the said   , on the   day of   , in the year aforesaid, through the inclemency of the weather and the want of the common necessaries of life, and by no violent ways or means whatsoever, to the knowledge of the said jurors, did die.

In witness, etc. (*finish with attestation as at page 61*).

Natural Death.

Copy caption as at page 61) that the said   , on the   day of   , in the year aforesaid, and for a long time before, did labour and languish

8

under a grievous disease of the body, to wit, an asthma, and on the said   day of   , in the year aforesaid, the said   , by the visitation of God, in a natural way, of the disease and distemper aforesaid, and not by any violent means whatsoever, to the knowledge of the said jurors, did die.

In witness, etc. (*finish with attestation as at page 61*).

Found Dead.

(*Copy caption as at page 61*) that the said   , on the   day of   , in the year aforesaid, in a certain field, situate at the   of   , in the county aforesaid, was found dead; and that the said   had no marks of violence appearing on his body, but, by the visitation of God, in a natural way, and not by any violent means whatsoever, to the knowledge of the said jurors, did die.

In witness, etc. (*finish with attestation as at page 61*).

Found Dead; Cause of Death Unknown.

(*Copy caption as at page 61*) that the said man, to the jurors aforesaid unknown, on the   day of   , in the year foresaid, in a certain wood called   , situate at the   of   , in the county aforesaid, was found dead; and that the said man, to the jurors aforesaid unknown, had no marks of violence appearing on his body; but how or by what means he came to his death, no evidence thereof doth appear to the said jurors.

In witness, etc. (*finish with attestation as at pag

By Excessive Drinking.

Copy caption as at page 61) that the said   ,
on the   day of   , in the year aforesaid,
by excessive drinking, and not from any hurt,
injury or violence done or committed to the said
          to the knowledge of the said jurors, did die.

In witness, etc. (*finish with attestation as at
page 61*).

Death in Prison.

Copy caption as at page 61) that the said   ,
being a prisoner in the prison aforesaid, on the
          day of   , in the year aforesaid, at the
prison aforesaid, by the visitation of God, in a
natural way, to wit, of a fever, and not otherwise,
did die.

In witness, etc. (*finish with attestation as at
page 61*).

CHAPTER 23.

1 Geo. V.

An Act respecting Coroners and Coroners' Inquests.

Assented to 24th March, 1911.

HIS MAJESTY, by and with the advice and consent of the Legislative Assembly of the Province of Ontario, enacts as follows:—

1. This Act may be cited as *The Coroners Act.* (*New.*)

2. In this Act, ''Coroner'' shall include Associate Coroner.

PART I.

APPOINTMENT OF CORONERS.

GENERALLY.

3.—(1) The Lieutenant-Governor in Council may appoint one or more Coroners for the whole or any part of every county, city, town, provisional judicial district and provisional county. See R.S.O., 1897, c. 97, s. 1 (1).

(2) This section shall not apply to the City of Toronto. (*New.*)

SPECIAL PROVISION AS TO THE CITY OF TORONTO.

4.—(1) The Lieutenant-Governor in Council may appoint a Coroner, to be called the Chief Coroner, and such number of Associate Coroners as may be deemed proper, for the City of Toronto.

(2) An Associate Coroner, subject to such regulations as the Lieutenant-Governor in Council may prescribe, shall perform all the duties and exercise all the powers of a Coroner.

(3) Except the Chief Coroner, every Coroner and Associate Coroner, appointed for the County of York, including the City of Toronto, shall have, exercise and perform within the City of Toronto only such powers and duties as are assigned by the regulations to an Associate Coroner.

(4) The Chief Coroner shall be paid in lieu of all fees by the Corporation of the City half-yearly, such salary not exceeding $1,500 per annum, as may be fixed by the Lieutenant-Governor in Council, and the Corporation shall be reimbursed out of the Consolidated Revenue Fund to the extent of one-half such salary. (*See* 3 Edw. VII., c. 7, s. 22, *part.*)

NOTICE OF APPOINTMENT.

5. A copy of the Order in Council appointing a Coroner shall be sent to the Clerk of the Peace of the County or District in which the Coroner is to act, and shall be filed by him in his office. (See *The Coroners Act*, 1887 (*Imp.*), c. 71, *s.* 12(3).

PART II.

INQUEST ON DEATH.

DISQUALIFICATION OF CORONER.

6. A Coroner shall not conduct an inquest upon the body of any person whose death has been caused at or on a railway, mine or other work, whereof he is the owner or part owner, or which is owned or operated by a company in which he is a shareholder, or in respect of which he is employed as medical attendant or in any other capacity by the owner thereof, or under any agreement or understanding direct or indirect, with the employees at or on such work. R.S.O., 1897, c. 97, s. 7.

DUTY OF CORONER ON INFORMATION OF DEATH.

7.—(1) Where a Coroner is informed that there is within his jurisdiction the body of a deceased person, and that there is reason to believe that the deceased died from violence or by unfair means, or in consequence of culpable or negligent conduct of others, or under such circumstances as require investigation, he shall issue his warrant to take possession of the body, Form 1, and shall view the body and make such further enquiry as may be required to satisfy himself whether or not an inquest is necessary. (See R.S.O., c. 97, s. 2.)

(2) After the issue of such warrant, no other Coroner shall issue a warrant or interfere in the case except under the instructions of the Attorney-General or the Crown Attorney. *New*.

8. If, after marking such enquiry, the Coroner deems it necessary that an inquest should be held, he shall issue his warrant, Form 2, for the holding of an inquest, and shall forthwith transmit to the Crown Attorney a statutory declaration, Form 3, setting forth briefly the result of such enquiry, and the grounds upon which he deems it necessary that an inquest should be held. (See R.S.O., c. 97, s. 6 (1).)

9. If, after viewing the body and making such enquiry, the Coroner deems an inquest unnecessary, he shall issue his warrant, Form 4, to bury the body, and shall forthwith transmit to the Crown Attorney a statutory declaration, Form 5, setting forth briefly the result of such enquiry and the grounds on which the warrant has been issued. (See R.S.O., c. 97, s. 6 (1).)

(2) Notwithstanding such declaration, the Attorney-General or the Crown Attorney may direct the Coroner making the same, or some other Coroner having jurisdiction, to hold an inquest upon the body, and the Coroner to whom such direction is given shall forthwith issue his warrant for an inqu

10. If the Coroner declares an inquest to be unnecessary and an inquest is not held by him, he shall be entitled for his services to a fee of five dollars and mileage at the rate of 20 cents per mile for every mile necessarily travelled by him, and such fee and mileage shall be paid in the same manner and upon the same conditions as the fees of a Coroner in a case in which an inquest is held. (See R.S.O., c. 97, s. 6 (3).)

WHEN INQUEST COMPULSORY.

11. Where the death of any person appears to have been in the construction or operation of any railway, street railway or electric railway, the Crown Attorney, subject to the provisions of section 6, shall direct a Coroner having jurisdiction in the locality to hold an inquest upon the body of the person so dying, and the Coroner shall issue his warrant and hold an inquest accordingly. (See 3 Edw. VII., c. 7, s. 22, *part*.)

12.—(1) Where an inmate of a house of refuge or house of industry dies, the superintendent, or other officer in charge, shall immediately give notice of such death to the Crown Attorney.

(2) On receipt of such notice the Crown Attorney shall enquire into the facts, and if, as a result of such enquiry, he is of opinion that such death took place under circumstances requiring an investigation, he shall direct a Coroner having juris-

diction to hold an inquest upon the body of the deceased person, and the Coroner shall issue his warrant, Form 2, and hold an inquest accordingly. (See R.S.O., 1897, c. 97, s. 3.)

13. Where a prisoner in a gaol, prison, house of correction, reformatory or lock-up dies, the warden, gaoler, keeper or superintendent thereof shall immediately give notice of such death to a Coroner having jurisdiction in the county, city or town in which such death takes place, and the Coroner shall issue his warrant, Form 2, and hold an inquest upon the body. (See R.S.O., 1897, c. 97, s. 3.)

POWERS AND DUTIES OF CROWN ATTORNEY OR COUNSEL FOR ATTORNEY-GENERAL.

14.—(1) Every Coroner, before holding an inquest, shall notify the Crown Attorney of the time and place of holding the same, and the Crown Attorney may, and if directed by the Attorney-General shall, attend the inquest, and may examine or cross-examine the witnesses thereat, and the Coroner shall summon such witnesses as the Crown Attorney directs. R.S.O., 1897, c. 97, s. 5.

(2) The Attorney-General may be represented by Counsel at any inquest, and such Counsel shall have the same powers as the Crown Attorney has under sub-section 1. (*New.*)

MEDICAL WITNESSES AND POST MORTEM.

15.—(1) The Coroner may at any time before the termination of the inquest, by his warrant, Form 6, direct a *post mortem* examination to be made by a medical practitioner with or without an analysis of the contents of the stomach and intestines.

(2) A *post mortem* examination shall not be made without the consent in writing of the Crown Attorney unless an inquest is actually held. (See R.S.O., 1897, c. 97, s. 12.)

(3) Every medical practitioner making a *post mortem* examination shall make a report thereon in writing upon a form approved by the Lieutenant-Governor in Council, which shall be supplied by the Coroner. *New.*

(4) No fees shall be paid to a medical practitioner for a *post mortem* examination unless such report is made and contains the particulars required by the form or satisfactorily accounts for their absence. *New.*

16.—(1) The Coroner may issue his warrant, Form 6, for the attendance before him or at the inquest of the legally qualified medical practitioner, if any, who attended the deceased at his death, or during his last illness, or of any other legally qualified medical practitioner in or near the place where the death occurred, but he shall not without the consent of the Crown Attorney order the attendance of more than one medical practitioner. (See R.S.O., c. 97, ss. 11, 12; *The Coroners Act (Imp.)*, c. 71, s. 21 (1).)

(2) A legally qualified medical practitioner shall be entitled for each attendance in obedience to any such order to $5 and mileage at the rate of twenty cents per mile for every mile necessarily travelled, and for a *post mortem* examination without an analysis of the contents of the stomach or intestines he shall be entitled to a fee of $15, and if with such analysis to an additional fee of $25.

(3) The number of miles so travelled shall be proved by the statutory declaration of the medical practitioner. (See R.S.O., 1897, c. 97, s. 14.)

JURY.

17.—(1) The number of jurymen to be summoned to serve on an inquest shall be not less than seven nor more than twelve.

(2) An inquisition may be found by a majority being not less than seven in number of the jurors sworn. *New.*

18. Where an inquest is held in a Provisional Judicial District the Coroner may, with the consent of the Crown Attorney, hold the inquest without a jury. *New*

19. A person shall not be qualified to serve as a juror unless he is named in the voters' list of the municipality and marked therein as qualified to serve as a juror. (See R.S.O., 1897, c. 97, s. 8.)

20. An officer, employee or inmate of a house of refuge, house of industry, hospital, asylum, or charitable institution, gaol, prison, house of correction, reformatory or lock-up, shall not be qualified to serve as a juror at an inquest upon the body of any person whose death occurred therein. (*New.*)

21.—(1) Every juror serving at an inquest shall be entitled to $1 for every day upon which such inquest is held and is continued for not more than four hours, and where the time occupied by an inquest on any day exceeds four hours, one dollar in addition for each such day and mileage at the rate of ten cents per mile for each mile necessarily travelled from his place of residence to the place where the inquest is held. (See R.S.O., 1897, c. 97, s. 16 (1). *Amended.*)

(2) Subject to the provisions of section 23, the amount to be paid to jurors shall be certified by the Coroner, who shall make his order for payment thereof. R.S.O., 1897, c. 97, s. 18 (2), *part.*

PAYMENT OF EXPENSES.

22. The Coroner shall give to every person entitled to fees, mileage or other expenses in connec-

tion with an inquest, an order on the treasurer of
the county, or of the city or separated town in which
an inquest is held, or in the case of an inquest in
a Provisional Judicial District upon the treasurer
of the district, for the payment thereof, and upon
presentation of the order the treasurer shall pay,
the amount named therein.   (*New.*)

EXPENSES OF INQUEST WHEN CAUSE OF DEATH TAKES PLACE OUTSIDE CITY OR TOWN.

23.—(1) Where an inquest is held upon the
body of a person who has died in a county, city or
separated town and the jury find that the cause of
death did not arise within such county, city or town,
the Coroner shall make an order for the payment
of the fees and expenses in connection with such
inquest on the treasurer of the county, city or town
in which the inquest is held, who shall thereupon
pay the same; and the amount so paid, shall on de-
mand be repaid by the treasurer of the county, city
or separated town in which the matter causing the
death is found to have arisen or taken place.

(2) In this section "county" shall not include a
city or a town separated from a county for municipal purposes.   4 Edw. VII., c. 10, s. 78.

ANNUAL RETURNS.

24.—(1) Every Coroner shall on or before the
15th   rn to

the Attorney-General for the year ending on the 31st day of December next preceding, containing

(a) Every case in which after investigation by him an inquest was deemed unnecessary, and

(b) Every case in which an inquest was held by him, with the findings of the jury, thereon.

(2) The return shall as far as possible show the name, place of residence and occupation of the deceased, the place of death, and the cause of death as found by the Coroner on such investigation, or by the jury at the inquest. (See R.S.O., 1897, c. 97, s. 19.)

(3) The return shall be in the form prescribed by the Lieutenant-Governor in Council which shall be furnished to all Coroners. *New.*

FEES OF CORONERS.

25.—(1) The fees and expenses to be allowed and paid to a Coroner holding an inquest upon a death shall be those set forth in schedule "A" and shall be payable in the first instance by the city or county and the city or county shall be recouped for the same out of the Consolidated Revenue Fund.

(2) The tariff of fees under the heading of "Coroners," the items therein being numbered from 1 to 8, in Schedule "A" to *The Administration of Justice Expenses Act*, is repealed.

(3) The list of charges payable out of the Consolidated Revenue Fund under the heading of "Coroners" in Schedule "C" to the said Act is repealed. *New.*

PART III.

INVESTIGATION OF FIRES.

ON REQUISITION OF INSURANCE COMPANY OR MUNICIPAL COUNCIL.

26. Where a Coroner within whose jurisdiction a fire has occurred, whereby any building, or any moveable property, has been wholly or in part consumed or damaged, receives

(a) A requisition in writing signed by the agent of an insurance company setting forth the facts as far as known, and stating that there is reason to believe that the fire was the result of culpable or negligent conduct or design, or occurred under such circumstances as in the interests of justice and for the due pro-ation;

and requiring the Coroner to hold an inquiry into the cause and origin of the fire; together with a statutory declaration that the statements made in the requisition are true to the knowledge of the person making the declaration; or

(*b*) A resolution passed by the council of the city, town, village or township in which the fire took place, that there are strong special and public reasons why an investigation should be held into the cause and origin of the fire and stating such reasons, and

(*c*) An undertaking on the part of the insurance company or council to pay the expenses of the inquiry,

he may in his discretion issue his warrant for summoning not less than 7 nor more than 12 of the householders resident in the vicinity of the fire to hear the evidence that may be adduced concerning the same and to render a verdict under oath according to the facts, or he may hold the inquest without a jury. (See R.S.O., 1897, s. 275, ss. 1-3.)

FEES OF CORONER.

27. Where an inquest is held by a Coroner in respect of a fire, the Coroner shall be entitled to the sum of $10, and should the enquiry extend beyond

9

one day, then to $10 *per diem* for each of two days thereafter and no more. R.S.O. 1897, c. 275, s. 7. *Amended.*

PAYMENT OF EXPENSES.

28. The insurance company or municipal council requiring the inquest shall alone be responsible for the expenses of and attending the same, and the fees, mileage and other charges shall be certified by the Coroner, who shall give his order in writing upon the company or the treasurer of the municipality, as the case may be, for payment thereof to the persons entitled thereto, and the same shall be payable accordingly. R.S.O. 1897, c. 275, s. 8. *Amended.*

29. The expenses consequent upon an adjournment of an inquest shall not be chargeable against or payable by the insurance company or municipal council requiring the investigation unless the Coroner has certified, under his hand, why and for what purpose in his opinion an adjournment took place or became necessary. R.S.O. 1897, c. 275, s. 10.

WHO TO BE PARTIES TO INVESTIGATION.

30.—(1) A director or officer of any fire insurance company interested, or the assured, or any person claiming under a policy of insurance, or any person prejudicially affected by any of the evidence add   el any investigation held under this Part as party thereto and may, with the Coroner's consent, examine, cross-examine or re-examine witnesses, as the case may be. R.S.O. 1897, c. 275, s. 12.

(2) The Coroner shall summon such witnesses as he may deem necessary and as may be required by any party to the investigation. *New:*

DISQUALIFICATIONS.

31. A Coroner who is a director or officer of the insurance company, or who is interested in any way, shall not hold an investigation under this Part, nor shall any such director or officer or any other interested person act for the Coroner as clerk reporter or otherwise in taking down or recording the depositions or evidence. R.S.O. 1897, c. 275, s. 13.

PART IV.

PROVINCIAL CORONERS.

32.—(1) The Lieutenant-Governor in Council may appoint Provincial Coroners, each of whom shall be by virtue of his appointment a Coroner for every county, provisional county and provisional judicial district for the purpose of
    (a) holding fire inquests,
    (b) holding investigations in cases of maiming or suspected poisoning of horses, cattle and other domestic animals, and

(c) holding an investigation in any case in which there is in his opinion reason to believe that property has been destroyed or damaged by the wilful or malicious use of explosives.

(2) Except where otherwise expressly provided, a Provincial Coroner when holding an inquest or investigation shall have all the powers of a Coroner.

(3) Where a fire has occurred whereby any building or any moveable property has been wholly. or in part consumed or damaged, and it appears to a Provincial Coroner that there is reason to believe that the fire was the result of culpable or negligent conduct or design, or occurred under such circumstances as require investigation, he may hold an inquest as to the cause or origin of the fire, and may summon a jury for that purpose as provided by section 16, or may dispense with a jury as he may deem expedient.

(4) A Provincial Coroner may hold an inquest or investigation without or upon the like requisition as in the case of a Coroner acting under Part III., but he shall not enter upon any inquest or investigation without the consent of the Attorney-General or the Crown Attorney.

(5) Where a Provincial Coroner acts upon the requisition of an agent of an insurance company, or   il, the

expenses of and incidental to the investigation shall be borne and paid in the same manner as in the case of an inquiry by a Coroner, and in other cases such expenses shall be borne and paid in the same manner as in the case of an inquest upon the body of a deceased person. *New.* See R.S.O. 1897, c. 275, s. 113; 7 Edw. VII. c. 23, ss. 10, 11.

PART V.

GENERAL PROVISIONS.

APPLICATION.

33. This Part shall apply to every inquest and investigation held by a Coroner or by a Provincial Coroner under the authority of this Act or of any other Act or law in force in Ontario. *New.*

WITNESSES AND EVIDENCE.

34.—(1) In addition to any other powers which he may possess a Coroner shall have the same power to issue summonses to witnesses, Form 8, to enforce their attendance and to punish for non-attendance or refusing to give evidence as is possessed by the High Court. *New.*

(2) A fine imposed for non-attendance or refusal to give evidence shall not in the case of a medical practitioner exceed $40, and in the case of any other

witness shall not exceed $10.   See R.S.O. 1897, c. 97, s. 15. *Amended.*

35.—(1) The evidence upon an inquest or any part of it, with the sanction of the Crown Attorney, may be taken in shorthand by a stenographer who may be appointed by the Coroner, and who before acting shall make oath that he will truly and faithfully report the evidence; and where evidence is so taken it shall not be necessary that it be read over to or signed by the witness, but it shall be sufficient if the transcript is signed by the Coroner and is accompanied by an affidavit of the stenographer that it is a true report of such evidence.   8 Edw. VII., c. 33, s. 29, *part.*

(2) The Coroner shall certify what he deems a reasonable allowance for the fees of the stenographer, and the same shall be paid on the order of the Coroner in the same manner as the other expenses of the witnesses.   10 Edw. VII., c. 26, s. 1.

(3) The sanction of the Crown Attorney to the employment of a stenographer shall not be necessary in the case of an inquest held by a Provincial Coroner or in the case of a fire inquest where one of the parties thereto in writing requests the Coroner to employ a stenographer and agrees to pay the extra charges occasioned thereby.   Now

INTERPRETERS.

36.—(1) A Coroner may, and if required by the Crown Attorney shall, employ a person to act as interpreter at an inquest, and such person may be summoned to attend the inquest.

(2) An interpreter shall be paid for his attendance and services such fees as may be fixed by the Provincial Coroner or by the Coroner with the approval of the Crown Attorney. 8 Edw. VII. c. 33, s. 30(1) *part.*

PENALTY ON JUROR FOR NON-ATTENDANCE.

37. Where a person duly summoned to serve as a juror does not attend, the Coroner may impose upon him a fine not exceeding $4.

RECOVERY OF FINES.

38. Where a fine is imposed by a Coroner under this Act he shall thereupon make out and sign a certificate stating the name, residence and occupation of the delinquent, the amount of the fine imposed and the cause of the fine, and shall transmit such certificate to the Clerk of the Peace of the county in which the delinquent resides on or before the first day of the General Sessions of the Peace then next ensuing, and the fine so certified shall be estreated, levied and applied in like manner and upon and subject to the like powers, provisions and penalties as if it had been a fine imposed at the General Sessions. See R.S.O., 1897, c. 97, s. 9 and *part* 10.

RETURN OF INQUISITION.

39. Every Coroner shall forthwith after an inquisition found by or before him, return the same, and every recognizance taken before him, with the evidence and exhibits, to the Crown Attorney. R.S.O. 1897, c..97, s. 18.

COURT ROOM FOR INQUEST.

40.—(1) The Council of every city and town shall provide a suitable place for the holding of inquests, and until it is provided for that purpose, inquests may be held in the Police Court room of the municipality, but at such times as shall not interfere with the use of such court room for the holding of the Police Court.

(2) If a suitable place is not provided by the council, the Coroner may procure a suitable place for holding the inquest and the expense incurred shall be borne by the municipality. 5 Edw. VII. c. 15, s. 1.

FORMS.

41. The forms set out in Schedule B may be used for the purposes therein designated but no inquisition shall be set aside or quashed on account of any deviation from any of such forms, where the instrument in question has been duly signed and attested, and the effect thereof is the same as that set out in the form provided for the purpose. *New.*

REPEAL.

42. Chapters 97 and 275 of the Revised Statutes of Ontario, 1897; section 22 of *The Statute Law Amendment Act,* 1903; section 78 of *The Statute Law Amendment Act,* 1904; section 1 of the Act passed in the Fifth year of the Reign of His late Majesty King Edward VII., chaptered 15; sections 10 and 11 of *The Statute Law Amendment Act,* 1907; sections 29 and 30 of *The Statute Law Amendment Act,* 1908, and section 1 of *The Statute Law Amendment Act,* 1910, are repealed.

43. This Act shall come into force and take effect on, from and after the 1st day of May, 1911.

(*For special provisions as to Coroners when acting under The Sheriffs Act,* see 9 Edw. VII. c. 6, ss. 14-16.)

(*As to Fatal Accidents in Mines,* see 8 Edw. VII., c. 21, s. 163.)

SCHEDULE A.

(*a*) Impanelling a jury ....\$ 2.00
(*b*) Examining each witness (including
          summons) 50
(*c*) Taking each recognizance 50
(*d*) Necessary travel per mile 20
(*e*) Taking inquisition and making return. 10.00
(*f*) Every warrant *l:.3:.4:.5:*...........   1.00
(*g*) Order for the payment of jurors 1.00

(New.)

SCHEDULE B.

FORM No. 1.

Coroner's Warrant to Take Possession of Body.

Province of Ontario, } To the Chief Constable of
        of   the   of   in the
      To wit: County (*or* district) of .

By virtue of my office these are in His Majesty's name to charge and command you that on sight hereof you forthwith take in charge the body of   , deceased (*or* the body of an unknown person) now lying dead at (*describing as accurately as possible the locality in which body lies*).

And thereafter do and execute all such things as shall be given you in charge on behalf of our Sovereign Lord the King touching the death of   , and for so doing this shall be your sufficient warrant.

Given under my hand and seal this   day of   , 19   .

                                                      ~   ner.

FORM No. 2.

Warrant to Hold Inquest on Death.

Province of Ontario, { To the Chief Constable of
of { the of in the
To wit: { County (*or* district) of .

By virtue of my office these are in His Majesty's name to charge and command you that on sight hereof you summon and warn (*not less than* seven *nor more than* twelve) able and efficient men of your county (*or* city) personally to be and appear before me on day the day of at o'clock in the noon of the same day at , called or known by the name or sign of , situate in the said then and there to do and execute all such things that shall be given them in charge on behalf of our Sovereign Lord the King touching the death of , and for so doing this shall be your sufficient warrant; and that you also attend at the time and place above mentioned to make a return of the names of the persons whom you shall have so summoned and further to do and execute such other matters as shall be then and there enjoined you and have you then and there this warrant.

Given under my hand and seal this day of , 19 .

Coroner.

FORM No. 3.

Declaration of Coroner that Inquest Necessary.

Province of Ontario,
of
To wit:
} I,   of the   of
in the   of   a
Coroner in and for said
      do hereby solemnly
declare:

That after viewing the body of   (*or* the body of an unknown person) now lying dead at   , in this   , I am of opinion that there is good reason for believing that   (*or* an unknown man, woman *or* male *or* female child) now lying dead at   , did not come to his (*or* her) death from natural causes, or from mere accident or mischance; but came to his (*or* her) death from violent or unfair means, or culpable or negligent conduct of others, or under other circumstances requiring investigation by a Coroner's inquest.

And I make this solemn declaration conscientiously believing it to be true and knowing it is of the same force and effect as if made under oath and by virtue of *The Canada Evidence Act.*

Declared before me at the   of
      in the   of   , this
      day of   , 19   .
}

Coroner.

A Commissioner, etc.

Form No. 4.

Warrant to Bury After a View.

Province of Ontario, of To wit:	To the person in charge or control of the burying grounds in the and to all others whom it may concern.

Whereas, an inquisition hath this day been held upon view of the body of , who now lies dead in your (township *or* city *or as the case may be*). These are therefore to certify that you may lawfully permit the body of the said to be buried; and for your so doing this is your warrant.

Given under my hand and seal this day of . , 19 .

Coroner.

Form No. 5.

Declaration of Coroner upon Order for Burial.

Province of Ontario, of To wit:	In the matter of deceased.

I, , Coroner of the of , in the County of , do solemnly declare that I visited and examined the body of the said and learned from the following facts:—

Upon these facts I issued an order to bury the body.

And I make this solemn declaration conscientiously believing it to be true, and knowing that it is of the same force and effect as if made under oath and by virtue of the Canada Evidence Act.

Declared before me at the   of ⎫
        in the   of   , this   ⎬
    day of   , 19   . ⎭

A *Commissioner, etc.*

FORM No. 6.

Warrant to Medical Practitioner.

Province of Ontario, ⎫ To   , a legally quali-
        of   ⎬ fied medical practitioner
    To wit: ⎭ of the   of   ,
                          in the   of   .

By virtue of my office these are in His Majesty's name to charge and command you that you do (make or assist in making a *post mortem* examination of the body of   , now lying dead at the   of   , in the County of   , without an analysis, and) appear before me and my jury at   , in the   of   , on the   day of   , 19   , at   o'clock, and give further evidence touching the death of   .

Given under my hand and seal this   day of   , 19   .

Coroner.

The words between the brackets ( ) may be omitted when a *post mortem* examination is not required.

FORM No. 7.

Summons to a Juror.

Province of Ontario, ⎱
      of ⎰
   To wit:

By virtue of a warrant under the hand and seal
of   , His Majesty's Coroner for this
of   of   , you are hereby summoned personally
to be and appear before him as a juryman on the
       day of   , at   o'clock,   in the
      precisely, at the   , known by the name
or sign of   , in the   of   , then and
there to enquire, on His Majesty's behalf, touching
the death of   , and further to do and execute
such other matters and things as shall be then and
there enjoined you, and not depart without leave.
    Herein fail not at your peril.
    Dated the   day of   , 19   .
    To   , of   , in the   .

Constable.

FORM No. 8.

Summons to a Witness.

Province of Ontario, ⎫ To   , of the
      of ⎬   of   , in the
   To wit: ⎭   of   .

Whereas I am credibly informed that you can
give material evidence on behalf of our Sovereign
Lord the King, touching the death of   , now
lying dead in the   of   , in the said
County of   . These are, therefore, by virtue

of my office, in His Majesty's name, to charge and command you personally to be and appear before me at (*here insert a sufficient description of the place where the inquest is to be held*) in the said   at   of the clock in the   noon, on the   day of   , and then and there to give evidence and be examined, on His Majesty's behalf, before me and my inquest touching the premises.

Given under my hand and seal this   day of   , 19   .

Coroner.

INDEX

Chief Coroners Card

Date

Name :

Apparent age

Address

Place where death
occurred Street No &c)

Form of enquiry held
Inquest   Investigation

What was death due to

Was this from natural
causes accident or Design

If by design was it suicide
manslaughter or murder

New
Born

CPSIA information can be obtained at www.ICGtesting.com
Printed in the USA
LVOW111300100313

323543LV00004B/150/P

9 781177 947978